How Coffee
Saved My Life

For the people of Lascano, Uruguay
Especially the Allio Silvera family

How Coffee Saved My Life

And Other Stories of Stumbling to Grace

ELLIE ROSCHER

CHALICE
PRESS
ST. LOUIS, MISSOURI

Cover image: Patrick Strattner /fStop /GettyImages
Cover and interior design: Elizabeth Wright

www.chalicepress.com

10 9 8 7 6 5 4   13   14   15   16

Print: 9780827214569 EPUB: 9780827214699 EPDF: 9780827214705

Library of Congress Cataloging-in-Publication Data

Roscher, Ellie.
  How coffee saved my life : and other stories of stumbling to grace / Ellie Roscher.
  p. cm.
  ISBN 978-0-8272-1456-9
  1. Roscher, Ellie. 2. Christian biography–Uruguay. 3. Spiritual biography–Uruguay. I. Title.
  BR1725.R67A3 2009
  278.95'083092–dc22
  [B]   2009023932

Contents

Acknowledgments

Countless thanks flow out as so many helped to make this project happen. I offer heartfelt thanks to the lovely, generous people of Lascano, especially the Allio Silvera family, for teaching me so much about grace and love, showing me God in a new culture, and shaping for me a more complex vision of home. To Tom, Andrew, Rob, Brooke, Christine, and Alyson: We will always be world champs. Thank you for being life-giving friends.

Thanks to Chalice Press for taking a chance on a new writer—especially my editor, Dr. Trent Butler. Also, to my parents, for providing and equipping me with everything so that I could logistically volunteer abroad for a year of my life. Unending thanks to my Daniel, for loving me so much that constructive criticism was not even an option. For holding me, literally and figuratively, during my year in Uruguay. For all those who have acted as consultants, cheerleaders, and advisors, especially Andy Brown and Dan Lee for improving my manuscript, Claire Bischoff and Shelly Talcott for saving my proposal, and all those who read my newsletters and encouraged me to keep writing. Specifically to Mary Hess, who would not let me take no for an answer and helped me navigate the writing world. You gave me a sense of vocation during a confusing time in my life. Finally, thanks to my phenomenal siblings and friends, who ground me and keep me laughing.

Preface

If you have come to help me, you are wasting your time. But if you have come because your liberation is bound up with mine, then let us work together.[1]

AN ABORIGINAL AUSTRALIAN WOMAN

Anytime an experience is transformed into words, it becomes a story. This is my story: how an experience came through my senses, filtered into my brain, dissolved into my heart, and was reincarnated as words. It is not the whole story, but it gets to the truth of my experience.

How can a year-long adventure come to life on a page? Among the countless stories I could have chosen, an endless number of people I could have introduced, a seaful of joys and sorrows I could have related, these are the parts of the story I chose to share. Being able to keep the rest of the experience to myself produces strength and wonderment, a jewel I will keep in my pocket, just for me, to accompany me on the rest of my journey.

It is a challenging process to write the in-the-moment truth and the truth in hindsight simultaneously in one story, conveying both authentically. Although I am conveying a year in my life, I did not want to write it like a textbook, but like a story. Being abroad can be disillusioning, and at times I lost faith in my ability to decipher what was truly happening. My hope is that my words will bring forth the essential truth of the story, that for one moment you too may feel what was real to me, that the truth will resonate inside of you, that you will find solidarity in the story and with the people. I hope that you can learn along with me in the story, bringing my experience to whatever context you find yourself in.

I chose the title *How Coffee Saved My Life: And Other Stories of Stumbling to Grace* because in Uruguay I stumbled my way into relationships that taught me the meaning of divine grace. I experienced the physical consequences of entering into relationships with people. I did not drink coffee before I left, but, for physical reasons, I was forced to while I was there. My coffee drinking became a metaphor for the whole year. In a new culture, the confident, put-together North American in me broke down to pieces. I stumbled through the year awkwardly, and God caught me with the expansive and generous grace I have come to know and love in a new, tangible way. Things as little as a cup of coffee and as unimaginable as divine love literally carried me through, and I am a new person for it.

I broke the book up into loosely chronological chapters made up of a combination of essays that include hindsight and raw journal entries from my year in Uruguay. Each chapter fits under a spiritual theme, showing how these values were made real through living them. I experienced things such as *hospitality* and *grace* at a new depth and intensity. Although I think we all grow from experiences of *vulnerability,* I would not wish experiences of *brokenness* on anyone. With that said, my entire year in South America transformed me.

Each vignette has a Spanish title. Even with college courses in Spanish, I still essentially had to learn the language during my time abroad. Not being able to communicate verbally was a contributing factor to my vulnerability. Here, I offer thoughts and use stories to demonstrate how I came to understand my new vocabulary and my new way of life. I hope you enjoy walking with me for a bit.

> Tonight was different. I felt like we were each separate and full to our edges with our own stories, mostly unshared. In a way it scared me, having a summer of experiences and feelings that belonged to me alone. What happened in front of my friends felt real. What happened to me by myself felt partly dreamed, partly imagined, definitely shifted and warped by my own fears and wants. But who knows? Maybe there is more truth in how you feel than in what actually happens.[2]
>
> Ann Brashares

Commissioning

While living for a few months in one of the "young towns" surrounding Lima, Peru, I first heard the term, "reverse mission." I had come from the North to the South to help the poor; but the longer I was among the poor the more I became aware that there was another mission, the mission from the South to the North. When I returned to the North, I was deeply convinced that my main task would be to help the poor of Latin America convert their wealthy brothers and sisters in the United States and Canada...

This "reversal" is the sign of God's Spirit. The poor have a mission to the rich, the blacks have a mission to the whites, the handicapped have a mission to the "normal," the gay people have a mission to the straight, the dying have a mission to the living. Those whom the world has made into victims God has chosen to be bearers of good news.[1]

HENRI NOUWEN

1

¿Porqúe?

"The America way of life" is simply not sustainable. Because
it does not recognize there is a world beyond America. But
fortunately, power has a shelf life. When the time comes, maybe
this mighty empire will, like others before it, overreach itself and
implode from within... Another world is not only possible, she's
on her way. Maybe many of us won't be here to greet her, but on a
quiet day, if I listen carefully, I can hear her breathing.[2]

ARUNDHATI ROY

I decided to go to Uruguay because I wanted to be interesting. Everyone I knew who had lived abroad embodied this creativity, this intentionality of living, this sense of being part of a whole that I wanted.

Mike came back from two years in Honduras and continued his bucket showers and bike riding, acutely aware of how we often overconsume resources.

Erin returned from India a vegetarian who grew her own lettuce in her sustainable garden and collected extra bagels once a week so they would not be wasted.

Kelly, after making lifelong friends in South Africa, went to political protests to swing opinions on bills that affected civilians in places she had never been.

I wanted the life stories of friends across the world to push me to construct a life of integrity in the United States. Here, I find it easy to live a life that constantly exploits people we have never met before, and I wanted to live with a sense of the rest of the world. I wanted the complexity of thought and maturity that emanated from these world-traveling gurus I knew. I have always believed in the interconnectedness of the global community. I knew that my daily actions affected people in other parts of the world. But I knew that to combat the pull toward a convenient lifestyle of power and privilege, I needed to live with a people, let them seep into my soul. I had traveled. I had seen the world. But the two-week trips I had previously taken to Guatemala and Trinidad, even when I strayed from the beaten path, left me feeling eager for deeper understanding and relationship. I hated being the obvious North American with the digital camera, baseball hat, and all-too-white tennis shoes. It was time to dig in my heels. I wanted to live with a people and be changed.

I decided to go to Uruguay because I wanted to slow down. I lived a fast-paced life because I was good at it, although I did not enjoy it. Although I knew it to be false, part of me still acted like my identity was intimately tied to my accomplishments. I was what I did, so the more I did, the more I was. At the moment I was signing up to go to South America, I was reading every word assigned to me in my master's program, writing a thesis, being a part of three active committees, working thirty hours a week, training for a marathon, and maintaining a healthy dating relationship and all-too-many friendships. I slept five hours on a good night, seeing things such as eating and sleeping as optional. Leisure time made me feel uncomfortable. I felt that I was on the verge of a catastrophic crash. The floor was creaking, and would soon fall out from under me.

I actually had recurring dreams of getting fatally sick or being in a car accident, something that would allow me to slow down and concentrate on what is important without people thinking me lazy. I wanted an excuse to come to a crashing halt. I wanted to be offered an alternative lifestyle, a creative alternative to the United States' rat race so I would not continue to run it forever. I had heard from these traveling friends that life in other countries was slower, and I had seen this on short-term trips with my own eyes. I wanted to live slowly in a community where living slowly was accepted, encouraged, and necessary. I wanted to try it on for size and maybe bring a love of my new pace back with me to combat societal pressure to do the contrary. I was tired, and I wanted to be comfortable living in North America with a non-North American pace of life without feeling guilty. I hoped living in a place that offered another lifestyle would build habits that would be contagious in my home country.

I decided to go to Uruguay because I knew that, if I did not intentionally insert myself into situations where I was the minority, it would never happen naturally. I wanted to be the other, the "least of these." Our communities in the United States have very little compassion for people who seem different from those holding power. I look at people who do not speak English as a first language or who get stares for their race or sexual orientation and wonder what I can do to help build a sense of relationship and community with them. I wanted to know what it felt like to not speak the language and not have the safety net of the majority to fall back on. I knew that it would be hard, but I had no idea what that "hard" would look like.

Safe in the U.S. where we have the illusion of control over such things, I looked forward to really experiencing everything. The part of me drawn to adventure and travel could not wait to go and, finally, truly live. If I had known beforehand the extent of the suffering that going would involve, I might not have gotten on that plane. After twenty-five years of living with the ease of power and privilege, trying to survive without it proved very difficult.

I discovered the depth of loneliness and hardship. I discovered what it felt like to live with the elements. The people in Uruguay say that they just feel everything more. The heat, without air conditioning or ozone to protect, is completely consuming and forces the pace of life to slow without exception or mercy. The humid cold, without heaters or insulating snow, seeps into the bones of the people and refuses to falter for months at a time. Yes, the heat and the cold were more extreme than I could wrap my head around. But so was every emotion that ran through my body.

I came to know hot, cold, surrender, brokenness, sickness, vulnerability, isolation, silence, loneliness, and hardship like never before. But my story is not a tragedy. After all my expectations were thwarted and I learned to really live in Uruguay, I also came to know grace, empowerment, hospitality, strength, courage, patience, and love with a transformational power and depth. I cried harder that year than I ever have. But that sorrow and disillusionment opened up room in my heart for deeper and truer laughter and joy.

Now that I have returned to a country where my race, class, and language give me the advantage, I still cannot fathom what it is like to struggle daily on the outside of privilege for a lifetime. I discovered that even with the hardest and most painful of lessons, my story was not a tragedy. This is my story in all of its beauty. This is a story of a woman who, in a single day, went from being an articulate English speaker to stumbling through broken Spanish. From eating bagels to eating cow tongue. From sleeping five hours a day to ten. From having three jobs to having none. From feeling successful and powerful to feeling like a useless, invisible failure. From being surrounded by friends to traveling by herself. From feeling graceful and in control to stumbling to grace on unknown soil. These are the transformational Uruguayan adventures of a rich North American overachiever.

August 2, 2005
The tears continue, which is odd for me. I am having real, unshakable doubts about this thing. Why do I have to leave? Why do I think it has to be hard to be good? I am so scared and so sad. The excited moments come less often. I don't know why I am doing this. I can give you all the stock answers, but it neither comforts nor helps. I had mouth surgery last week and have been miserable ever since. The doctors have stopped treating Courtney's cancer and are waiting for her to die. I look into Dan's eyes and wonder what I will do without him for a year. I have spent a lot of time downsizing, simplifying my life to a travel pack. I wonder if I am exaggerating or being dramatic, but I think I have reason to be both sad and scared. Why am I doing this to myself? To my friends? To my family? Why is Courtney dying? It always has to be hard so I can grow, but maybe there is growth in staying still. Maybe that will be one of my lessons.

Duele

At no time are we ever in such complete possession of a journey, down to its last nook and cranny, as when we are busy with preparations for it. After that, there remains only the journey itself, which is nothing but the process through which we lose our ownership of it.[3]

Tukio Mishima

A week before I left for Uruguay, my friend Courtney Lynn Walker died of cancer. She was a dear friend, a roommate from college, one of the most spirited, talented, and beautiful women I have ever had the privilege of knowing. In the end, she had only wanted her very closest souls in, including my roommate at the time, Shelly, who was her very best friend. My role was second-string support, being strong, and coolly passing information onto the third string. I saw Courtney a few months after her diagnosis, when I flew to Washington, D. C., to spend a weekend with her, and then not again until a week before she passed.

Shelly told me it would be okay to intrude on family for a day to come say good-bye, so I calmly put my packing down and asked my boyfriend, Dan, to drive me to South Dakota. Courtney had come home to die. We pulled up to her driveway in Madison, South Dakota, and took a deep breath before knocking on the front door. Seeing Courtney, bloated in some places and eaten away in others, a barely functioning twenty-five-year-old, I sped as casually as I could to the bathroom thinking I would surely puke in the sink. I stayed bent over, gasping for breath for some time, gathering the strength to face reality again.

Cancer had quite literally eaten her alive. In a daze I moved around the house with the family. We ate food, watched movies, moved her body when she needed to get more comfortable, and gave her pills, hoping we were in a nightmare that would become a happy ending in the morning. They let me sit with her by myself as I searched her mutated body to find the gorgeous, talented, and spunky woman I loved. I suppressed all the anger, the pain, the confusion, so that I could soak my last moments with her conscious self up into my soul to pull out when I needed her most. She somehow came out of her semi-comatose state to say, "I love you, too," very clearly as I was leaving her for the last time. Dan drove the whole way home so I could collapse in pain in the passenger seat. I spent most of the ride in the fetal position with my head in his lap, willing sleep to take reality away.

She died two days later. I did not work to get past the shock, knowing that an unending well of sadness was waiting at the end of the numbing paralysis. I continued about my business of packing and saying temporary good-byes in attempts to deny reality. Dan and I turned back around and drove to South Dakota for the funeral within the week, only four days before my departure. The whole trip was a daze. I only remember talking to old friends, crying in the choir loft during the ceremony, and being devastated for her three younger siblings. I was too busy remembering to breathe, disillusioned with grief, dizzy with loss.

I was no less dizzy when I got on a plane to go to orientation, wondering when I would break and let myself feel the loss of her presence. I feared being far away from anyone who could help me keep her alive through story. I feared not having the language skills to express my pain. I feared I would find few people to trust enough to help me hold my grief. I left for Uruguay with heaviness in my heart, without the time to begin to process. I left with the desire to be around people I loved and with the fear of losing someone while I was gone. In hindsight, I think Courtney would have been proud of me for getting on that plane with my heart that exhausted with loss.

October 7

I wanted to tell my North American self, owner of running shoes and detergent, "Welcome to the world." I wanted to feel the weight of my

American history on foreign soil. I wanted to listen and learn in hopes of returning a more grounded, intelligent, worldly woman who is also a hopeful, relevant, responsible, and sensitive citizen of the world. I wanted to sneak past that coastal guard and work my spoiled butt off for justice and human rights while being gently, ever so gracefully presented with a different way of life. And by all means, I wanted to leave room for my imperfections.

Orientación

Go to the people
Live among them
Learn from them
Love them
Start with what they know
Build on what they have
But the best leaders
When their task is done
The people will remark
"We did it ourselves."[4]

CHINESE POEM

I was leaving so much in Minnesota to go live in South America for a year. I had an amazing family, a loving boyfriend, fabulous friends, a great job, a stimulating intellectual community, a dynamic church, and a healthy network. My good-byes were extremely difficult, prolonged and exhausting. Many people were excited for me, but their lives would barely be affected by my absence. I was leaving everything and everyone that I knew. The waiting was painful and agonizing. The unknown loomed and consumed. If I had gone from the good-bye parties straight to my volunteer site, I might have actually died from culture shock. I do not think that any human being could go from such abundance of relationships and comfort to such scarcity without long-term damage. Luckily, I had two orientations to help me through the transition process.

The first was a week-long orientation in Chicago with all the volunteers in the young adult programs in both the ELCA and PCUSA churches. The hardest part of the whole session was actually getting on the plane that went to Chicago. As soon as I got there, the ELCA church kept me too busy to be nervous. Besides, it felt so good to end the waiting. The Lutheran and Presbyterian programs comprised sixty-seven volunteers and a good number of facilitators. We formed a strong community. Basically, the first stage stripped me of my friends and family, but offered me the comforts of being in the United States. We still enjoyed comfortable beds, enjoyable conversation in English, the Internet and phones in case we needed to get in touch with home, good food—the works.

To get cleared to go to Uruguay, I had to pass a series of physicals. I have been blessed with good health, so I didn't expect any problem. My first pap smear a month before I left had come back irregular, but that happens to women all the time. I left for Chicago before hearing the results of my retest, taking the doctor's advice not to worry. A few nights into orientation, I used a phone card to call Dan, who started the conversation by telling me to call my mom. She informed me that I had to come home. The second test had also come back irregular. My melodramatic self immediately flashed to Courtney's fight with cancer, and I felt a rush of grief thinking I may not be able to leave the country.

After all that buildup and summoned courage, it seemed cruel that I would have to stay. I started to cry with frustration thinking of having to say good-bye to Dan and my family again. My heart was well on its way to leaving, and this was a horrible step back. I heard a knock two seconds after I hung up and found a friend standing outside, with his last name, "Papp," staring at me from the upper lefthand corner of his hooded sweatshirt. I started to laugh as I explained the coincidence.

I spent the next morning booking a flight and setting up an appointment back home. The gynecologist treated me for what he thought was wrong, causing very painful cramping. He told me to go to Uruguay; and if the results came back differently than he expected, I could always come back home. I enjoyed seeing my family and boyfriend one more time, but not a single tear was shed the second time at the airport. This hiccup, this interruption, had focused my desire to go. I was thankful for my health and lucky for the opportunity. I realized that I was more excited than scared, but it took the possibility of not going to help me see that.

I came back to find that between the volunteers and the staff, an estimated seventy-five near-to-complete strangers were praying for the health and well-being of my vagina. It was slightly awkward and precious all at once. A few weeks into my Uruguayan adventure, I was informed that I should get a checkup when I came home, but that I was free to stay in South America for the rest of the year.

My second orientation was in Buenos Aires, Argentina. I sensed small changes. Sixty-seven volunteers had become seven; the English became Spanglish. I started getting exhausted from trying to understand informational sessions in Spanish, but we could still take a break at night and debrief in English with the other volunteers. The location became foreign. The faucet read F for *frio* and C for *calor*. The food, dress, seasons, rotation of the toilet water, and pace of life were all different. Information was hurled at us about the history of the country and the Church, cultural differences, geography, the subway system, human rights violations, wine, and the tango. We traveled the city and listened. We slept a lot and prayed.

The most interesting thing we did during orientation was march with the mothers and grandmothers of the "disappeared" in Plaza de Mayo. The head of the group, Nora, informed us that during the 1980s dictatorship, over 30,000 citizens in Argentina simply disappeared due to political or theological leanings. Often, late at night, masked men would break into houses and take people who were never seen again. Of the 30,000, only 250 bodies have been found. Some had washed ashore, suggesting the ocean no longer wanted to be an accomplice. Some headless bodies had sunk to the bottom of the ocean with cement blocks tied to their feet, forming an underwater graveyard. An estimated 500 children were taken from disappeared women after birth and given to wealthy families of the military, who took special pride in stealing babies from politically liberal parents and raising them "right."

After marching with the women for a half hour, we were taken back to the office to speak with Nora. Nora is well under five feet, compassionate, intelligent, and articulate. She is full of hope, energy, and passion. She wore a white kerchief on her head symbolizing the diaper of her son. In a sea of faces on the wall, Nora pointed out a picture of her son, who had disappeared when he was twenty-four. He was politically minded and thought of as subversive to the dictatorship. Nora has been marching with other mothers of the disappeared in Plaza de Mayo every Thursday for over twenty years. The government refuses to hand over any information, leaving thousands of families without emotional closure or deserved explanation. The silence is deafening. She told us that new lawyers get put on the case now and again, but stop getting paid if they begin to uncover too much. The mothers want justice. They want answers. They want closure.

I learned about the dictatorships in Chile and Uruguay as well. The Chilean dictatorship made no attempt to hide all its murders of progressive thinkers. Although the violence was unbearable, families were given the opportunity to know the truth and mourn the loss. In Uruguay, the dictatorship was not as violent, but still managed to infest a community with fear. Few were murdered, but thousands were imprisoned. It did not affect my rural town much, but a few co-workers of Tom, the volunteer in Montevideo, had spent up to twelve years in prison, one just for being a teacher.

We frantically tried to soak in all that was being thrown at us. We had naïve ears, eyes, and hearts that we desperately tried to keep open and engaged so that we could understand our new environment and adjust, becoming relevant guests. Processing new information in a new context was hard work, but it was invigorating, too.

Between the time I took the flight from Minneapolis to Chicago and the day I arrived at my placement site, almost a month passed. Part of me was anxious. It was time to go and make my mistakes. But I was also very grateful to have time to adjust to each stage of the immersion process until I was equipped to embrace the adventure on my own.

August 24
If the rich contribute something, they have to receive something in return. Leadership should always come from the inside. I seek engagement, not to save them, but to make me more whole. I am us. This is our story. Walk with. Listen. Engage actively. Share. Build community and fellowship. Witness.

Casi

Patience is not a waiting passivity until someone else does something. Patience asks us to live the moment to the fullest, to be completely present to the moment, to taste the here and now, to be where we are. When we are impatient we try to get away from where we are. We behave as if the real thing will happen tomorrow, later, and somewhere else. Let's be patient and trust that the treasure we look for is hidden in the ground on which we stand.[5]

HENRI J. M. NOUWEN

I thought it all made sense back when I thought it needed to all make sense. Life should be continuous, every career move building on the next, ultimately landing a job that is financially secure while making the world a more beautiful place. It was not acceptable to stray from the path, lose sight of the goal, or, heaven forbid, do something just for the sake of fun without having a reason. Going abroad was always a dream of mine, but it wavered on a selfish decision that might not make perfect sense with the bigger plan. That doubt, coupled with the events of 9/11 during my senior year of college, pushed me to sidestep the adventure, possibly forever. I worked at a shelter in Denver and got my masters, so everything was making sense. But I could not shake the desire to go abroad. I sensed the optimal time had come for me to break up the college, masters, good job, house with a white fence, 2.4 kids and a dog, retirement track, etc. I thought I just might be able to do it in a way that continued to make sense. I started looking seriously for an abroad volunteer program that could fit.

Watching my friends go off to countries like Kyrgyzstan and Nepal with the Peace Corps and struggle with the isolation of a rural area and a four-day walk from the nearest North Americans, I looked for programs that would put me in a city and give the support of other volunteers in the community. I found one that made sense. The ELCA's Young Adult Program sends volunteers all over the world. They accepted me into the program in Argentina. I would be able to improve my Spanish, which would help me in North American urban settings. A community of volunteers would live in Buenos Aires, one of the biggest, most dynamic urban cities in the world. It all made perfect sense. When I told people in my life, it made sense to them, too. Professors, family, and friends all congratulated me and agreed that this would not be a waste of a year, but one that would enhance my journey. They could see how this would be a logical move that would build my resume and supplement my career neatly and nicely. Most of us feel more comfortable when things make sense.

By the time I arrived with the six other volunteers in Argentina for a ten-day orientation, we knew that Andrew from South Carolina, Rob from Arizona, Alyson from Wisconsin, Brooke from Alabama, and Christine from Minnesota would all be in Buenos Aires. Tom from Illinois would be in the capital of Uruguay, Montevideo. And I, a city girl with a masters in urban ministry, would be heading to a place in rural Uruguay that few, if any, people in the United States have ever heard of. Getting my placement over e-mail, I did struggle a bit with not knowing why I was going anymore or what was in it for me. The unknown loomed with the illogical and discontinuous while I packed. But only during orientation in Argentina did the absurdity of my placement site finally sink in fully.

I realized that I could not lean on logic or rationality to write off my crazy move to South America. I would not be building my resume. Our site coordinator handed me a small piece of paper with my new address on it. It read:

Ellie Roscher c/o Marcelo Nicolau
Montaldo s/n casi Dr. Corbo
27300 Lascano
Rocha
Uruguay

s/n stands for *sin numero*–without number. *Casi* means almost. Montaldo without number, almost Dr. Corbo. I would not be in an urban hub with friends a bus ride away. I would be twelve hours from them, and my town was so small, I did not even have an address. My house was on a street called Montaldo, almost at Dr. Corbo. Was Dr. Corbo another street name? So I was near an intersection? Were there intersections? Did I live close to the town doctor? Did Dr. Corbo go on house visits because there were too few people to have a hospital? No one knew. But my romanticized visions of doing urban ministry abroad came crashing down. Why were they sending the workaholic urban queen of North America to a town without addresses? I started to breathe deeply trying to recreate my expectations.

I realized how much I would miss community. The six other volunteers helped me laugh about my address, as we turned *casi* into our tag word. To help us deal with the fact that reality did not in any way mirror our expectations, we would throw the word *almost* in, always leading to laughter that honored the surrendering process.

After the Argentine volunteers spent a weekend with their new house families, we laughed until we had sore abdominals reliving each person's culture shock moments. Brooke's shower, consisting of a single trickle of running water, *almost* had as much water pressure as a drinking fountain. Later she *almost* dodged being painfully and explosively sick from the meat they had for dinner. Alyson *almost* beat her two-year-old "brother" at soccer. Andrew found himself stumbling through Spanish at a Pentecostal church. He hoped that he *almost* said, "I am glad I am here. Thank you. Praise God." He sat in his new room and thought he might *almost* not make it through the night alive, wondering whether he was suffering from culture shock or carbon monoxide poisoning emanating from the space heater in the corner, since both bring on fatigue, headache, and disorientation. And Rob, the storyteller of all storytellers, recounted being *almost* mugged, as he was abandoned at a film group full of German-speaking atheists in the most dangerous neighborhood in the city.

I wondered whom I would laugh with when reality finally hit for me, when I first saw my address-less home, or the first time I *almost* enjoyed cow tongue for lunch. Over dinner the seven of us transitioned gracefully from subjects of theology to politics to pop culture to anxiety about the year. We shot each other looks from across the room when asked to do seemingly bizarre things in this very foreign country. We checked in with each other as our bodies, minds, and spirits began the process of culture shock.

This was my first lesson in surrender. My placement, being *almost* what I signed on for, would never make sense, no matter how hard I tried. It took me months to realize that it did not have to. Holding that address in my hand was the moment I began the scary, challenging, beautiful process of letting Uruguay into my heart. To do so, I had to let go of what I thought were wants and needs, what I thought made sense and what I thought would build my resume. *Casi* became my tag word, what I went back to when I was struggling to let go of expectations. As I became more comfortable with the knowledge that I was not in control, I began to realize I never really was to begin with. The more I let go of expectations and started to celebrate the *almost,* or more often the *not even close,* the more Uruguay offered me grace and abundance. Maybe, just maybe, it did not need to make sense to be good and right.

> You will make all kinds of mistakes, but as long as you are generous and true and also fierce you cannot hurt the world or even seriously distress her.[6]
>
> WINSTON CHURCHILL

Vulnerability

In 2001, just a few weeks after the 9/11 attacks, the Jewish community celebrated the harvest festival of Sukkot. Many did so by building a sukkah—a fragile hut with a leafy roof, the most vulnerable of houses. Vulnerable in time, since its roof must be not only leafy but leaky enough to let in the starlight and gusts of wind and rain.

In our evening prayers throughout the year, just as we prepare to lie down in vulnerable sleep, we plead with God, "Spread over us Your sukkah of shalom—peace and safety."

Why does the prayer plead for a sukkah of shalom rather than a temple or fortress or palace of shalom, which would be surely more safe and more secure?

Precisely because the sukkah is so vulnerable.

For much of our lives we try to achieve peace and safety by building with steel and concrete and toughness:

Pyramids, Air raid shelters, Pentagons, World Trade Centers.

But the sukkah reminds us: We are in truth all vulnerable. If as the prophet Dylan sang, "A hard rain's gonna fall," it will fall on all of us. And on 9/11/01, the ancient truth came home: We all live in a sukkah. Even the wildest oceans, the mightiest buildings, the wealthiest balance sheets, the most powerful weapons did not shield us.

There are only wispy walls and leaky roofs between us. The planet is in fact one interwoven web of life. The command to love my neighbor as I do myself is not an admonition to be nice: It is a statement of truth like the law of gravity. However much and in whatever way I love my neighbor, that will turn out to be in the way I love myself. If I pour contempt upon my neighbor, hatred will recoil upon me.

Only a world where all communities feel vulnerable, and therefore connected to all other communities, can prevent such acts of rage and mass murder.

15

The sukkah not only invites our bodies to become physically vulnerable, but also invites our minds to become vulnerable to new ideas. To live in the sukkah for a week, as Jewish tradition teaches, would be to leave behind not only the rigid walls and towers of our cities, but also our rigidified ideas, our assumptions, our habits, out accustomed lives.

By leaving our houses, we create the time and space to reflect upon our lives… For we have built a culture that has little space for the sukkah of reflection, of hospitality to new, uncomfortable ideas, as it does for the sukkah of vulnerability and physical discomfort.[1]

ARTHUR WASKOW

Lascano

Take long walks in stormy weather or through deep snows in the fields and woods, if you would keep your spirits up. Deal with brute nature. Be cold and hungry and weary.[2]

HENRY DAVID THOREAU

Although the actual population of Lascano is 7,000, most of those people live on farms on the outskirts. About 2,500 people inhabit the central town. I immediately struggled with how closed off the small town felt. Some people were on the inside, but I was not one of them. The 2,500 inhabitants of the town numbered 2,450 more than I imagined when I received my numberless address. Lascano is located in Southeast Uruguay about two hours from the ocean and one hour from Brazil by car. The most popular tree is the palm, the most popular house pet is a cow, the most popular drink is *maté,* and the most popular modes of transportation are bikes and mopeds. Life was very slow, but very good.

The pastor and his wife—Marcelo and Marina— picked me up at the bus station and brought me to their house to meet my three new "siblings." My house family was absolutely precious. I had a thirteen-year-old sister Dinorah, an eight-year-old brother Santiago, and a four-year-old brother Ignacio. Marina and Marcelo are a beautiful team of equals in a very machismo town in a very machismo culture. Marina teaches grade school, and Marcelo pastors the Waldensian Church. I was there to help run an after-school program in which about thirty kids come to eat, work on homework, and play games. The kids there, like kids everywhere, were adorable and quick to love. They were absolutely enchanted with my blonde hair, white skin, and muscles on a woman. Marcelo and Marina explained to me that I would help with the youth group, Sunday school, and Bible studies at the church.

A late dinner of homemade pizza on the first night featured a get-acquainted time laced with awkward questions presented in my broken Spanish that used Mexican vocabulary and a Minnesotan accent, both of which were uncharted territory for my new house family. Afterward, I hid up in my room to gather myself. Reality sunk in. For months, I had been dreaming of my new town. The unknown was romantic, exotic, exciting, and beautiful. The reality was dirty, scary, foreign, and far away from home. That first night, tears loomed just below the surface as all the dreams fell away.

Expectations became reality. This is where I would spend the next year. I felt far away from everything I had known. I was petrified to the point of having to concentrate so I would remember to breathe. I did not know if I was up for this. I did not know where to go to find courage. I left everyone I loved to go to orientation in Chicago, then Argentina, then Montevideo. At each step, I was stripped of more comforts until I found myself totally and utterly alone in Lascano.

It was real. That first night, surrounded by introverted strangers who had no idea who I was or how to welcome me, I literally looked around and found nowhere to turn. I felt tangibly every mile that separated me from my family and every cultural barrier that separated me from the people I had just moved in with. In a blink of an eye, I had no power, no control. I was the *other*–a silent, vulnerable foreigner with not a single friend in the world. I, for the first moment in my life, felt my blonde hair, my blue eyes, my United States citizenship, and my first language. It was time to let my expectations shatter and be replaced by reality. It was time to set new goals. In the U.S., I imagined all the engaging I would do, how I would change and change others. I would be the best volunteer the ELCA Church has ever known. That night, my vulnerability became painfully evident. My goal became getting through my first night without sobbing.

I stayed in bed the first morning until 11 a.m., partially because of how tired I was from travel. Partially. The other part was that I was petrified. It would be months until my first thoughts of the morning were in Spanish. What should I do? What should I say? I slowly went downstairs with my journal and started writing, the hobby that would prove to be my saving grace. The baby step I had taken was that I was sitting in a space where I was sure to interact with someone eventually. Sure enough, Marcelo came and invited me to go on a driving tour of the town. I kept my eyes open wide and willed my heart to open as well. The car was barely in one piece: dirty, small, with torn upholstery and only partially working doors. Most of the roads were dirt and gravel with horrible potholes, promoting driving at about the pace of the bikers. The few paved streets were worse to drive on than the gravel ones. I noticed palm trees and abandoned buildings; only a few buildings in the whole town were two stories.

Kids and bikes loomed everywhere. The town was simply dirty and rundown. Unlike my experience in the capital, I found no political fliers or graffiti, no chain store signs or even evident businesses. People stared at me, long and hard. The town appeared to have no landscaping or color, no obvious culture or entertainment. It did have a plethora of stray dogs and wandering cows, fences and broken windows. Marcelo took me to different neighborhoods and pointed out the schools. We took about five minutes to drive from one end to the other of the long, thin town. Open cow fields and rice fields marked either side. What I saw was not the kind of poverty you would see on a TV commercial—no starving children with bulging bellies. I discovered only a subtle, rundown, rural economic struggle. No one lived on the streets, but countless homes were made of sticks. I would have to learn to call this town home.

In a couple of residential neighborhoods all the houses looked the same. One had houses that lined up in rows and ran along the rice packaging plant. They were painted white cement, one story with a very small living space, even smaller kitchen, a closet for a bathroom, and two to three bedrooms that each barely fit a bed. The insides always displayed mismatched furniture and plastic trinkets for decoration. Kids would play soccer in the narrow lanes between houses, and dogs would run free. Another neighborhood consisted of houses about the same size, very utilitarian, but made of brick. People living in these two neighborhoods were the middle class. A few more-extravagant homes housed privileged people such as the head of the rice packaging plant. Many homes made of tin or sticks evidenced complete destitution. Marcelo told me that during the winter, when it became bitterly cold without heating systems, the houses of sticks and hay would burn down and have to be rebuilt several times.

Sprinkled in the streets of homes were storefront churches; two Internet cafes that each had six ancient computers for kids to play games on (and for me to send e-mail home); and homes that sold fruit, torta fritas, or trinkets out of the front for a living. One could find things such as clothes or a vacuum cleaner to buy, but most took a bus an hour to Brazil, or five to Montevideo, to shop a few times a year to capitalize on the city prices. The center of the town, like all Uruguayan towns, featured a square plaza with a statue of Artigas in the middle and benches where young people flirted and old people gossiped. The storefronts in the plaza included the bus stop, an ice cream parlor, the preschool, the Catholic church, their version of a dollar store, the butcher, and a push cart that sold cigarettes and fish.

I had never had to navigate a small town before, much less one on the other side of the world. This one contained no signs, no chains, and no hub of commercial life. It took me a few months to get my bearing and find places where I could mail a letter, make a phone call, or find a Coca-light.

My point person in Argentina must have talked to Marcelo before I arrived because he seemed to know things about me without me telling him. For one, someone had told him I was an athlete. It had been a few years since I had thought of myself as one, but the people of Lascano were simply fascinated with that part of who I used to be. During the first week of my time there, I found myself at the dinner table with three Spanish/English dictionaries—one mine, one Marcelo's and one Dinorah's—drawing pictures to try to get across what gymnastics was. Marcelo started including in his introduction of me to other people things such as the fact that I had run three marathons and competed in college sports. I knew something was being lost in translation when I would then be asked, "Have you ever been in the Olympics?" That first month, all I could really say to set them straight was, "No," knowing their imaginations were making me out to be a specimen that I never was or ever will be. Marcelo took me to the town gym during my first full day in Lascano. Far different from gyms back home in size, cleanliness, cute outfits, they had nothing like daycare, hot tubs, Pilates classes, or pools to offer. Reality further set in for me when I realized that I did not recognize a single court. I stuck to running with the cows for exercise until I was absolutely desperate enough for human interaction to enter the gym for class.

The sense that was most affected, to my surprise, was my sense of smell. My house always smelled like urine. During the cold months, I would put perfume on the inside of my scarf or turtleneck to ease the subtle yet suffocating power of the odor. The uneven and demolished sidewalk, if existent at all, made it so dangerously difficult to walk that most people opted for the middle of the dirt streets with so few cars as competition for the roads. This was also an advantageous location because running alongside the walk was always a mix of human waste and something green running over the litter that I never fully got used to the smell of. Lascano smelled of humidity, manure, dust, and any kind of waste you can think of. Do apathy, monotony, and fatigue have a smell?

Second to smell, Lascano rocked my sense of sound as well. White noise invaded my first few months. Unable to understand Spanish unless a kind, patient soul spoke directly to me, everything turned into white noise. I struggled mightily, as I deeply adore silence. All the sounds were strange: the spoken word, the music, the countryside, and the advertisements shouted at me as through a megaphone. I grew to hate the television. In Marcelo's house, it was on constantly. If Ignacio or Santiago were home, it was the sound of horrible (to me) Spanish voiceovers on the Cartoon Network lulling them into a stupor and filling them with literally hours of nothingness. Dinorah chose music videos with a beat and lyrics I failed to understand and with shockingly objectifying images of women that refused to stop. Marcelo chose soccer, which to me was the least of the evils. Although amused, I was not a fan of the nights that one soccer game was on television while another was on the radio. Welcome to South America.

Marina, who rarely took control of the TV, chose the news, which in Lascano was rarely earth-shattering. The only silence came when I slept or during the handful of times I was home alone that year. Otherwise, I endured a combination of Lascano radio—reporting about which eight-year-old soccer teams were playing that night, what time church was on Sunday, and how much a kilo of rice was being sold for—and the television with the screeching cartoon characters or Shakira undressing herself. I did not even understand either radio or television for the first four months. Even when I did begin to understand, it was trying.

I got through my first days calling up courage from moment to moment. I observed without understanding a word. Every now and then I would try to talk, each sentence a struggle, an embarrassment, a cry for help. I was herded around, never really knowing what was going on. I ate, slept, and breathed. Such automatic acts became victory enough. Arriving in winter made life that much more difficult. It never got quite cold enough to invest in heating systems. It never snowed. Still, I had never experienced a humid cold such as this, and I suffered greatly. I would wear long underwear and scarves indoors as well as out. I was lucky that our family had a fireplace and that Marina loved to have a fire going. I would get relief briefly at night reading with my feet almost touching the flames. I slept under blankets so heavy I could not roll in my sleep. Getting up in the morning was the last thing I ever wanted to do. The cold encouraged my isolation.

Slowly, my new reality started setting in. I began to thaw. I put a card a friend had sent to me on my nightstand. It read, "One day at a time." Each night, after somehow getting through another day, I would smile. That card willed me through the first few weeks. Success was redefined. Going from an abundance of friends, food, family, power, and comfort to none, my situation felt like a primeval struggle for survival. I coped with the feeling of survival by remembering the abundance. Eventually, reverse mission would take hold. Eventually, I would find abundance in Uruguay, too, but not at the beginning. At the beginning, Lascano felt scarce and scary.

In the United States, with my overbooked life, days and months flew by. But without work, family, friends, language, or a familiar matrix to live in, with no clear sense of purpose or path, minutes would creep by. Marcelo's family had a calendar on the wall in the living space with one vertical strip that had the months of the year and another that had numbers one through thirty-one. Using alternating primary colors, one would move a fish down on each strip accordingly so that the square in the fishes' stomachs would show the date. I remember moving the "date fish" every day in the month of September, needing a tangible sign of my progress, wondering how I would ever live to see the "month fish" travel all the way to next August.

A million little and big things heightened my senses and forced me to live slowly. I tried to tread lightly in my new town and observe differences in lifestyle without judgment, though my emotional reality seemed to make judgments uncontrollable. Every day was new and scary and exciting and exhausting. On the days when I felt too tired to let the new in, I reminded myself that this was the reason I came: to experience what life is like in another part of the world, but this challenge that I signed up for was daily and constant. I could take no days off. I could not return home for a brief holiday. The comforts were not here. I could not sleep in my old bed, speak English, see my friends, drive a car, or eat at my favorite restaurant for a year. For twelve months, I would go without feeling in control—as if I knew what was going on, or was totally at home. It took faith and pep talks to remind me that the payoffs of making this place my own would come for the rest of my life. This was a sacrifice that I had welcomed. I could not hide. I could not snap my fingers and fast-forward to the end of the year. The fish moved only once a day. I had to live every moment of it. The only way out was going through.

September 13
I feel isolated at the moment, but soon I will go see the town and the church and meet people. Then, over time, it will become my home. I will be able to run, do my yoga, go to work, go on walks… It will get better.

I am just trying to find peace until it unfolds. It is so funny how I react to stress and lack of control—find a place for all of my belongings, stop eating, search for routine, daydream of home, try to keep busy. Today I made a calendar of all the days until I return home so that I could see visual progress of my time left. It is hard to imagine that I will have a tough time leaving at the end of the year, but I am sure I will. Right now I am struggling with not being able to make a good first impression because I cannot speak the language. I don't know how to integrate myself without language, and Marcelo seems to lack the desire and patience and outgoing nature to help me get there. Then I have to laugh at myself for being melodramatic. This is my first full day here.

October 6

I have learned to laugh at myself without the help of the other volunteers. I laugh with anticipation of watching a year full of ridiculous surprises unfold. I can laugh at myself as I wave to the cows staring at me on my run as if they are old friends. I laugh at myself using the wrong verb tense and involved charades to get my idea across. There are still dark days when I do not understand, where laughter is not close to the surface, when I question my placement in Lascano with a pastor, when I want racial diversity or a coffee shop or the ability to escape, and it just does not seem funny at all. But most of the time, I can give a victorious little grin as I think, "So I am in Lascano…"

I have had time here to do things I never would have dreamed of doing in the United States: go for a walk by myself, journal every day, sit and do nothing besides let the paint on my nails dry, listen to a CD all the way through with no side activity. I wonder which, if any, I will make priorities back in the United States, or if I will go right back to the rat race.

October 12

I would guess I live in the nicest house of the seven volunteers. I definitely live in one of the nicer houses in town. It has a kitchen, sitting room, office, two bathrooms, and three bedrooms. We have running water and phone, a car, a scooter, and two TVs. I sensed that this must be extravagant here because when the youth group came over, they all walked around with wide eyes and gaping mouths telling my house parents how beautiful it was. Most of them live in one-story, cement homes. They all asked me if my house in the U.S. had two floors, and repeatedly asked me to tell what the inside of a plane looks like. As I get used to things like the smell of urine in the house and eating one substantial meal a day, I realize that for most in the area, I am living like a queen.

Simple

*The absolute desire of "having more" encourages the selfishness
that destroys communal bonds among the children of God. It
does so because the idolatry of riches prevents the majority from
sharing the goods that the Creator has made for all, and in the
all-possessing minority it produces an exaggerated pleasure in the
goods.*[3]

ARCHBISHOP OSCAR ROMERO

We collected our shower water in a bucket, and reused it to flush
the toilet once a day. We composted, but we did not recycle. Salad
consisted of eggs, rice, and potatoes. When the sink turned on, the
shower turned off. I did not see a diamond ring, iPod, laptop, SUV,
or chain store. We never, ever, threw food away. More people owned
and used bikes than cars. DVD players were shared in town, carried
from house to house. We dried our clothes and our hair with the sun.
We reused wrapping paper multiple times. The kids did not have
textbooks or folders, sports fields or computer labs. They paid for
photocopies that they glued into their notebooks rather than having
their own books. They went to school half the day, and everyone
wore uniforms. Teachers got paid more than the police. Dinner,
which was usually between 10 and 11 p.m., consisted of a glass of
milk and a little bread.

As I adjusted, I noted how little I used and consumed. In the first
two months, I wore one pair of shoes, two pairs of pants and three
shirts. I stopped wearing jewelry and make-up, and I only worked
two hours a day. The only purchases I made were bus tickets, fruit,
e-mail sessions, and a birthday gift for my house brother Ignacio. I
knew every person I handed money to personally and knew that
they benefited directly from my purchase. I began to believe in my
power as a consumer. The money in our economy, the little that there
was, stayed in our town instead of being shipped out for a CEO in
another part of the world to buy a third personal jet. I knew that the
fruit I bought helped my students go to school. The e-mail sessions
helped put food on the table. I walked everywhere. Everything I
owned here could fit in my travel pack. I was really thinking about
what I truly needed versus what I wanted. I found it refreshing to
be stripped of things and their hold on my identity. I welcomed the
adjustment, seeing how people live with less and think nothing of it,
never knowing any different.

The hardest part of coming home would be seeing people who have too much and don't realize it. People are not always creative with resources because they do not have to be. Our system is set up so that I can rarely guarantee who ultimately benefits from my purchases. I receive hundreds of messages daily from companies making me think that I have to buy something to be somebody. God help me if I slip deeper into a comfort and convenience that exploits other people. Shame on me if I have two houses while others have none. One of my friends, upon returning from the YAGM program in India, made it a goal to live a life in the U.S. that he would not be ashamed to show his new Indian friends if they ever did have the money to come see him. I think that is a fair goal: to live a life that is not shamefully excessive.

Simple living to me is a lifelong process of recognizing self as a member of the interconnected world community. It is committing to a movement toward a sustainable lifestyle that empowers others to do the same. Simple living is important because a false sense of entitlement can lead to economic violence and oppression of others who deserve to experience freedom as a part of their human dignity. It is important eternally because all humans are interconnected over time and space. The earth is mortal. Simple living is worthwhile because it is a civic duty. The freedom that comes with it brings joy and builds relationship. It serves ourselves, God, the cosmos, future communities, and the current world community. It involves valuing the dignity of other human beings and the cosmos by showing respect for all of creation. It requires a critical eye and mind; a desire for mutual relationship, consciousness, contemplation, intentionality; and a seeking heart.

Simple living is the ability to see energy and resources used to make a water bottle. Some countries do not have drinkable water. In other countries where water is drinkable, bottled water has become a manufactured need. North Americans do not need bottled water. In our town of Lascano, it had become an unfortunate necessity because of undrinkable natural water. Simple living is countercultural where I live now, in North America, but is a necessity in Lascano, Uruguay, where no one thinks twice about it because no one knows an alternative. Although it takes effort to not go along with the wasteful status quo of my current community, when I strive to live a simple lifestyle, one that does not diminish my happiness but respects the rights of others, I feel like I am honoring the people and the time I spent in Uruguay, when I finally realized that less can be more than enough.

December 11
    I feel limited in my ineffectiveness, inefficiency, silence, and uselessness. I have to sit in my nothingness, my disposability, my invisibility and dwell for a year until I truly believe there is worth in my inherent being as a person outside of my ability and productivity, how much other people need me. I am just God's child, and that is enough, even if I accomplish nothing else in life.

Preguntas

Have patience with everything unresolved in your heart and try to love the questions themselves... Don't search for the answers, which could not be given to you now, because you would not be able to live them. And the point is, to live everything. Live the questions now. Perhaps then, someday far in the future, you will gradually, without even noticing it, live your way into the answer.[4]

RANIER MARIA RILKE

Although I like getting answers at times, I have never minded lingering in the mystery and complexity of questions. Never in my life have I lived in questions more than I did in Uruguay. When I go back to my thoughts and feelings during that time, the questions and the feeling of questioning are pervasive. I usually worked about two to three hours a day when the kids had school. When they did not go to school, which was surprisingly often, I had a day with no work. In the United States, that would have been great. But in a small town where I had no friends or identity, it was a struggle for me. I endured a lot of time in my own head. I found many questions but few answers.

Why am I here?

How does this fit into my call?

If I sit and pray among the poor and become poor myself, will it make a difference?

Will God liberate the woman being beaten and the hungry children who are pimped out by their parents?

Will my tiny faith transform anything?

Will I learn Spanish here?

How can I incorporate this simplicity into my life in the United States?

Will my relationships at home suffer?

How do I humanize and show dignity to the beggars and the vendors in the city?

Why am I the sidekick of a pastor of a church I know nothing about?

What am I supposed to be learning?

Will I really make it without going nuts?

Am I too old to be at the whim of another family in a different hemisphere?

Will I ever stop counting the days left?

Will I ever stop being hungry?

Will I ever be given any responsibility?

Will they see my gifts, and will I step up and use them when the time is right?

Why was I given a site that clearly has no idea what to do with me?

How can I laugh instead of cry when ridiculous things happen to me?

Why is everyone surprised when they find out I am twenty-five?

Will I ever be able to communicate at a level where my personality can come through?

Why is it such an adjustment for me to not feel pretty or smart or respected?

I do believe relationship can help, but what will my presence really do? How can I relieve Lascano of a little of the hurt? They hurt so much, and I am just me. I see so much that money cannot fix.

It hurt so much to give up myself and my desires so completely. I wanted it to be easy. I wanted English and my friends and success and respect and food and space to call my own and a vocational call. And like a "good North American," I wanted it immediately.

March 4

"Traveling alone?" the remis (taxi) driver asked me.

"Yes," I said, and the reality of it almost choked me. I felt like I was literally and figuratively traveling alone.

Sola

You are living through an unusual time. You see that you are called to go toward solitude, prayer, hiddenness, and great simplicity. You see that, for the time being, you have to be limited in your movements, sparing with phone calls, and careful in letter writing.

You also know that the fulfillment of your burning desire for intimate friendships, shared ministry, and creative work will not bring you what you really want. It is a new experience for you to feel both the desire and its unreality. You sense that nothing but God's love can fulfill your deepest need while the pull to other people and things remains strong. It seems that peace and anguish exist side by side in you, that you desire both distraction and prayer concentration...

It is clear that something in you is dying, and something is being born. You must remain attentive, calm, and obedient to your best intuitions... You feel vulnerable but safe at the same time. Jesus is where you are, and you can trust that he will show you the next step.[5]

HENRI J. M. NOUWEN

During my year in Uruguay, I was laughed at and made to feel inadequate more than ever before. I had no skills in communication. I could not make friends or earn respect in the same ways I did in the United States. In my native tongue, I was good at listening actively, asking strategic questions, going deep in conversation, telling funny stories that endeared people to me, and offering compliments to make people smile. None of these things were possible in Spanish. I understood so very little, and what I could express was not theology and philosophy, but immediate and superficial things, such as the weather. I had become a painfully awkward lurker of sorts. Every day I had things that I wanted to say, but chose to stay silent because I could not find the words or courage to try to convey my thought in Spanish. It was awkward, but easier to be silent, to let things go unsaid.

No one knew what I was thinking or feeling, and no one seemed to care. After getting lost early in a conversation full of inside lingo and spoken too fast, I would remain in the space as a seemingly invisible and irrelevant observer. I felt very isolated and frustrated and useless. In this darkness, however, I found a deep dependence on God. I looked around to find my identity. Not having work or relationships to fall back on, I found my identity completely in God. One night I could not sleep due to doubt, loneliness, and under-stimulation. Not being able to earn or deserve love like I thought I previously could, I challenged God to stop loving me in my uselessness, ineffectualness, and unemployment; however, I was answered with a feeling of love.

I learned to celebrate small victories and joys in the day. Finding the post office, having a successful four-sentence conversation, admiring a sunset, or initiating an interaction became noteworthy. Being more dependent and more vulnerable, I learned what grace truly is. When a stranger welcomes me despite my stuttering, failing, vulnerable self and shows me love just because I am a fellow human on the journey, I have received grace.

On a Tuesday night early on, the church decided to throw me a welcome party. It was the first time I felt heard outside of interactions with my house family. The old women in the congregation made food. The kids from the after-school program brought pop. A fifteen-year-old named Jairo, who was impressed that I had remembered his name even though I could not pronounce it perfectly, had clearly showered and put on his collared shirt under his dirty work sweatshirt for the occasion. I hugged the kids I had met and thanked them for coming. We nibbled the traditional hors d'oeuvres, staying cautious around each other. Eventually, the church elders sat me down in the front for a question and answer session. I was petrified, but it went just fine. At times, Marcelo had to rephrase a question so that I could understand, already more able to communicate with me than strangers after just a few days of my living in his home. As I stumbled through my Spanish, they all hung on every word attentively, trying to sift through my thick accent and poor grammar. They knew nothing about me, but threw me a party anyway. Countless moments before that Tuesday, I felt utterly alone; but that day I realized that I was not. That is powerful. Grace waited there for me, and I was filled with gratitude. The welcome party continued to stand in stark contrast to the long, lonely nights of doubt. I learned in Uruguay that questions, doubt, and a sense of injustice are made out of the same substance as gratitude, joy, and goodness. All can be brought to God in worship; all can form a soul.

September 6
  Breathe. Pray. Do yoga. Try to poop.

Café

*I don't believe in charity. I believe in solidarity. Charity is
so vertical. It goes from the top to the bottom. Solidarity is
horizontal. It respects the other person and learns from the other. I
have a lot to learn from other people.*[6]

Eduardo Galeano

Have you ever been constipated for a few days? You just feel a little off, don't you? With it comes bloating, fatigue, and a heightened awareness of diet and bodily functions. But after a few days, we have learned to buy prune juice or take fiber supplements. Although the discomfort is not consuming, relief is welcome as we return to life as usual. Imagine, if you will, that lingering discomfort becoming a chronic plague. The entire time I lived in Uruguay, my body was in active revolt against me. It was the first time in my life that my body was estranged from me. But it did not stop at estrangement. It declared war. The next time you are feeling a little plugged up, imagine having to wait twelve months for relief. It was bad.

During my ten-day orientation in Buenos Aires, I thought that my "plugged-up-ness" was a fairly normal reaction to travel, change in diet, and schedule. Little did I know that this would be my permanent physical state until the day I returned to the United States. I began to take my situation seriously on day seven of no intestinal activity. I had not pooped in ten days. Every time I sat on the toilet, I waited, but got not so much as a hint that things in there were wanting to move, or even adjust. I had started to run and drink copious amounts of water to shake things up. My advisor bought me pears. Still nothing. I massaged my midsection and did yoga to no avail. I named my bowels Bertha. The bloating made me feel pregnant, in need of some "birth-ah." The pooping process had begun to resemble the difficulty of pushing something the size of a watermelon out a hole the size of a Clementine. I began talking to Bertha, gently persuading her to work with me. "Bertha, it is time," I would say with some gentle love pats. "Please wake up and wiggle. I do not want to explode." I continued to eat and get more and more grossed out as I pictured seven, then eight, then nine days of full meals just hanging out in my intestines. My stomach got taut. I felt overweight, pregnant with something much less cute and interactive than a young babe.

After the fruit, prayer, extra water visualization exercises and message, I set out one morning in my culturally insensitive running shorts and had to slow to a walk part way because of pain in my midsection. Without conscious effort, my body stopped, involuntarily moved to the curb, and proceeded to vomit water on to the street. I floated out of my body and saw a blonde freak in pink shorts puking all by herself in the streets of Buenos Aires. Awesome. I looked up to see that I was not, in fact, alone. A middle-aged Argentine man was curiously gawking at me as he swept the front stoop of his store directly across the street. I am not sure if it is possible, but I promise he was expressing reaction to my ashen-white legs, hot pink running shorts, blond hair, expensive tennis shoes, and the impressive volume of perfectly clear projectile vomit all at the same time. I was so plugged up that I was vomiting water in front of strange men. It was time to poop.

Before moving south, I had never had a single cup of coffee in my life. It was time to turn to the dark side. With fear of caffeine addiction, bad breath, stomach rot, and my dentist father judging my brown, stained teeth, I poured my first cup of coffee. A couple of cups later, I was wired and shaky; but I was wired and shaky on the toilet. It was quite possibly a miracle. I do not know if I can do justice to how great that first poop felt. It would be like if you lived for a week with an entire set of Legos lodged in your digestive track and then got them surgically removed. Or if the physical pain of overeating on Thanksgiving lasted two weeks and then was magically taken away. My mental, emotional, and even spiritual state instantly changed. I was figuratively and literally on the move again. I did not need to waste time and energy on issues of my large intestine. I could move on to more noble subjects, such as God, justice, and peace.

I thought that the momentum of the first coffee-driven poop would guide me to normalcy. It did not. The horrible process started all over again. I was yet again bloated, overweight, and concentrating on bodily functions that most people take for granted. Pooping is not something I wanted to bring up with my new house family. A new toilet that flushed with shower water once a day was not the place I wanted to be patient and pray to God for some relief. Within a few months, my daily breakfast had become two cups of black coffee and five fiber pills my mom had mercifully sent me. I began associating the smell of coffee with pure physical liberation. I became physically, mentally, and emotionally attached. I hated the taste of coffee and how it made my stomach feel, but it became completely necessary for my survival as I dreamed of regularity.

This is not a coffee romance like you see on Folgers commercials. My house family in Uruguay did not have whole beans from Guatemala with cute mugs, creamer, sugar, and hazelnut flavoring.

My coffee addiction was fixed by opening two individually wrapped packages of Nescafe and dumping them into a glass that was nuked for a minute and a half, then choked down. The burn in my stomach was nothing compared to the release of pressure of bulging bowels. Every once in a while, I would take a break to see if, indeed, my body had become at home in Uruguay. But, alas, I was constipated for an entire year of my life. It took a strategic combination of coffee, exercise, fruit, and prayer to win the daily battle, if not the war.

When agreeing to travel to South America for a year, I did expect to go through adjustments. But I naively assumed that my body would eventually give and become a member of my new community. I never imagined the physical struggles that would subtly chip at my spirit. It was one more way I was asked continually to give up the control that I was used to. Fruit was expensive and hard to come by. If we were lucky, we had apples and oranges available for dessert. It was a tough and embarrassing subject to address with my house family, and one that they did not easily understand. They had been born and raised on this red meat, low fiber diet. I never felt great, always aware of my foreignness. Constipation was more consuming than one might think, but that was just the beginning.

In addition to my constipation, I could not breathe through my nose for the first three weeks that I was there, as my body got used to a new climate and new wildlife. I have had my fair share of colds, but this was ridiculous. I wedged tissues up my nose for being so tired of blowing, as I dreamed of taking a drill to my head to release some of the pressure. They kept telling me I was reacting to the heat and the plants, which were depressingly inescapable.

I got lice. Several times. For a total of four months. I first noticed the nape of my neck burning, and by the time I ran a fine comb through my hair, I was infested so intensely that a louse tried to escape the comb via my forehead. The lice loved my head, declared my scalp their stomping ground, and dug their heels in for the long haul. Twice a day I combed through my annoyingly long, blonde hair, picking out the eggs one by one. I imagined the bugs crawling on me at night. Lice appeared in my town effortlessly, but even the locals were shocked at how often and how long I was plagued by the little critters.

I got mange—body lice. This ailment did not consume me physically and was not especially detrimental to my emotional well-being. I just thought with my previous place of residence and status I would be guaranteed a mange-free existence. While camping with my house family, a dirty dog came and brushed up against me, and

I knew it was over. The scalding summer heat made shorts the only humane option, but that left large surface areas of skin vulnerable to bugs, sun, and unidentifiable critters. I knew after one look at the dog that he was a carrier of things I did not want to acquire. Sure enough, little blisters spread on my legs for a month.

I burned from the sun until I blistered. I am an Irish American with fair hair, skin, and eyes. SPF 45 is a necessity daily in the United States, but only during the summer. Every day for a year, even in the middle of the winter, I put sunscreen on because Uruguay has less ozone, and I could feel the strength of the sun trying to cook me. I walked through the main plaza in Montevideo during winter wearing a hooded sweatshirt and jacket. The only skin showing was my face. Although I was freezing, I could feel the strength of the sun. Sure enough, I turned bright red and shed a few layers of skin the following week.

I gained *twenty-five* pounds. Even running every day, I could not maintain my healthy body weight. My body just was not used to the laid-back lifestyle and the high-protein, high-fat diet Uruguayans have known their entire lives. This was actually a big struggle for me. As a former gymnast, I have always been very conscious of my weight, and I associate unneeded body fat with imperfection. Although societal pressure was quite different, and there was no one I needed to impress, I did not welcome my extra curves.

This is just a small sampling of the physical challenges that my body dealt with during its war on constipation. These parts of my year introduced me to the Uruguayan culture in a very personal way. Mange, lice, and a strong sun are things that the Uruguayan people deal with constantly. They do not know any other way. Needless to say, I now totally believe in eating food native to where we were born. The people in Lascano had eaten red meat and whole milk their entire lives because they raised cows. They were perfectly healthy and fit. If they ate as much fruit and vegetables as I was used to, they would get sick with inspired bowels instead of stubborn ones. Coffee was not a necessary staple for them as it became for me. I just mourned the fact that my body continued to remind me loud and clear that I was not and may never be a true citizen of Uruguay.

If I were to have sheltered myself in hopes of steering clear of their ordinary food and their ordinary challenges like mange and lice, I would have missed out in some way. It would not have been as rich of an experience had I not gone through the cultural adjustments. These physical ailments and limitations broke me and made me vulnerable. They actually helped me build relationships as I had to ask for help, learn more about the culture, and laugh at myself. When I suspected I had lice, my house sister checked, confirmed, and showed me how to deal with it. She combed my hair daily, and I looked forward to the time we set aside to chat, even if her touching my head was to pull bugs out of my hair. These were the precious moments, when I was a bit broken and others let me lean on them in all my imperfection. Ultimately, these things made me feel tough, strong, and part-Uruguayan. They humbled me as a foreigner and forced me to ask for help and receive it graciously. Lice, sunburn, mange, and meat products were a part of life there, so I am glad that I went through it and truly entered into the community with my actual body.

I went to Uruguay because I believe in the world Church. I wanted to see God working in a different hemisphere. I wanted to fall in love with and serve a people who I did not previously know existed. God does not call us to love half way. Where God leads is not always pretty and fun, glamorous and exciting. Sometimes God calls us to lice and constipation. Those small challenges seem trivial now, looking at the love I have in my heart for the people of Uruguay. I am different now because I went to Uruguay with an open heart, ready to bear and share the reality of the people for a year. It comes out in little ways, such as the fact that I now eat with my fork in my left hand, that I live slowly enough to drink tea, that I can now speak two languages, and that I take the time to continue building relationships with my friends in Uruguay.

I do not only hold these people in my *heart*. Because we dared to love each other, I also carry them in my *body*. Discipleship carries physical consequences. I could not pretend to build relationship. Authentic relationship requires the commitment of mind, body, and soul; the stakes for a foreigner are raised. I was a stranger in a strange land. The consequences of that commitment can be both positive and negative. I learned to love big enough that people could see it as well as feel it. I now drink coffee socially, with no strategic consequences in mind. But it makes me think fondly of mornings in Uruguay when my heart and body were eager for relief.

December 7

I hate how much Marcelo yells. Sometimes during an awkward silence at lunch, I feel like he yells at one of the boys for something silly just to break the silence. He is inconsistent and mean. He sets them up to fail with lack of clear expectations. He yells more when he is tired and busy. It is a hard house to be in, especially knowing that it is probably one of the most peaceful in Lascano. I don't know how to help. I don't know how not to. He seems passive-aggressive and moody. I don't know what their expectations of me are, so I tiptoe around and try to be invisible and cautiously do the dishes or fold laundry when I can and sit in silence so as not to add to the chaos while he yells. It is difficult. Is it a cultural difference, or is it wrong?

Justicia

Injustice anywhere is a threat to justice everywhere. We are caught in an inescapable network of mutuality, tied in a single garment of destiny. Whatever affects one directly affects all indirectly.[7]

MARTIN LUTHER KING JR.

Originally I was frustrated that I was sent to a small town, when my training was for work in urban areas. What can a woman with a masters in urban ministry do in a town of 2,500? The issues in Lascano, though, were hauntingly similar to the inner cities of the United States.

The first weekend I was there, I went to a powerful workshop on domestic violence. A group in the church was trying to get trained and start talk around town so that women felt more safe getting help. Abuse of women was a pervasive problem there, as were child prostitution, alcoholism, and poverty. Most of these pervasive injustices were only talked about. The efforts took place behind very closed doors. Marina would point out women who she knew were being beaten or who had come to the church for help. One moment will stick in my throat whenever I think of domestic violence in Lascano.

I was walking from my house toward the middle of town and passed a house I knew well. This house on the corner sold plastic toys and pencils out of the front. Almost always, someone was hanging around in the back to offer a hello. On that particular day, the boy probably around seven-years-old was biking around the house. He had to slam on his breaks, went into a skid, and tipped over the bike and himself to avoid a passing car that he failed to see coming. I jumped with a start, but was glad to see that he was okay. His father had a different reaction. Maybe the father was scared his son almost got hit, or maybe it was anger at almost ruining the bike, or the embarrassment of people turning and staring, including the driver.

Whatever the major cause, something inside of the father snapped. He ran out, grabbed his son, literally dragged him to the house, and then kicked him inside. This all took about four seconds, during which time both parents started to raise their voices at the child as well. The boy's face mirrored pure terror, and the noises of dreaded anticipation that came out of his mouth as he was being dragged made me think this was not the first time something like this had happened. I froze, as did everyone around me. I had no idea what my role was, but I felt sick to my stomach, a coward, an ineffectual human being as I walked home with my heart in my throat, trying not to imagine what was going on inside that house.

Poverty was also pervasive in Lascano. Rural poverty looks different than urban poverty, but both are ugly and pervasive, similar in nature. Two kids who embody rural poverty for me are Augustine and Maria Eugenia. This precious brother and sister team were two of my favorite students (although I was not allowed to have favorites) at the rural school I taught at a couple of kilometers outside of town. Marina taught first through third grade in one classroom and the director taught fourth through sixth. Resources were limited, so for me to be able to come as a volunteer and teach them how to play was a treat for all of us. All they really knew how to do, growing up on farms, was work, and work very hard. Augustine was spunky, while Maria Eugenia was timid and sweet. Their parents had run into a string of bad luck financially a year back and moved out to the country, where they could live in poverty with more dignity. The neighboring families supported them by offering a cow and some chickens. The dad biked into town once a week, trailing the milk behind him to sell. Sometimes during the hot summer months the milk spoiled by the time he reached town, so the kids would drink the sour milk until the next week, the only sustenance the kids would receive apart from the lunch and snack the school offers. The kids borrowed a neighbor's horse and rode it to school. They had no electricity or plumbing. On days it rained, they stayed home from school and put all the furniture up on tables, knee high in water. Through their dirty clothes and faces, their eyes and smiles shone just the same.

Marina told me that the dirty, torn clothes they wore to school were their dress clothes, only used for school and church. What they wore at home was even worse. Another day at morning snack, Augustine, a growing boy, asked for a third huge cup of milk. Marina warned him that might be too much dairy for his stomach, but he told her he had not eaten since lunch at school the day before. A lot of kids lived like Augustine and Maria Eugenia in Lascano. I never saw anyone sleeping on the streets, because the town was small enough that people took care of each other, even if it meant moving out away from town a bit. Lascano had no homeless people, but painful stories of hunger and poverty abounded. The country had a lot of internal and external debt and offered very few jobs. Rural poverty has a different face than urban, but it is just as real and just as painful.

I was embarrassed, after only a month in Lascano, that I thought my urban training would go to waste in rural Uruguay. For one, I faced more hurt than I knew what to do with. For another, a second reality hit home. Theoretical issues in school become real people, real kids getting kicked and drinking sour milk. All my training seemed to fall through the cracks in an instant.

October 25
A thin line separates hope and despair. Today, I hope. I sit, letting the sun dry my hair, looking out on the gravel roads of the country. My heart is so content that I know I will learn something today, that I will be patient and vulnerable enough to surrender. Or maybe I will just exist in Lascano for a day, and that will be enough. I have crossed back over to hope today, seeing God in more things, more people, more moments, and I pray each morning that God holds me there gently and affectionately.

September 23
I believe that the opposite of love is fear. At the heart of oppression is fear: fear of change, fear of losing power and privilege and money and control. Believing this, I am trying to search my heart and dig out my fears. Why do I fear losing control? Why do I fear isolation and mediocrity? When I am running, I still fear the men driving trucks or staring. Why? I always have a little piece of me worried about my safety, and it bothers me because I am judging the other instead of trusting and loving. Why are people afraid of what is different? We miss so much because it is a little harder, a little less comfortable, a little less natural to connect with people who are different from us. I am fighting the instinct to judge people here for their differences as I am also trying not to judge people at home. I want to think critically and love compassionately.

Sangre

When we become aware that our stuttering, failing, vulnerable selves are loved even when we hardly progress, we can let go of our compulsion to prove ourselves and be free to live with others in a fellowship of the weak. That is true healing.[8]

HENRI J. M. NOUWEN

Some moments in Uruguay changed how I lived my life. Others taught me about God, justice, or even myself. *This* moment showed me, very simply, that during time spent abroad, something totally foreign *will* happen to you. The only way you can possibly deal with it is also foreign. Some moments bring no big lesson beyond that.

The fateful day happened in October, when constipation had taken a serious hold on my life. We had plans for the day that I did not understand at all, due to my lack of speaking the native language. What I thought I knew was that this Sunday in Lascano was La Criolla, the spring festival celebrating the breaking in of the horses. What? What is that? I did not know in the slightest. But I knew I was going. And I knew that the car was leaving at 10 a.m. Factoring in my lack of pooping, my plan for Sunday was to get up at 9, have some coffee and hopefully get Bertha moving before this trip out to the country. This plan was thwarted when no one decided to tell the English-speaking girl that Sunday was also the day that the time gets moved ahead. Not wanting to be rude, they let me get up at 9, which was actually 10, and then told me the car was leaving. No coffee. No pooping. Adjust.

I rushed into the car after my shower and was hauled off to the day of the horses. I was a little excited for the outing, even though I had no idea what a horse breaking festival consisted of. On the thirty-minute ride, I was hoping the discomfort starting in my midsection was my intestines crying. I got out of the car and realized, without a doubt, I had gotten my period unexpectedly. Awesome. I was in an open field, surrounded by strangers, most of whom are dressed like gauchos, with a severe language deficiency in a country that does not believe in tampons. So what did I do? Well, one option was to go around and ask complete strangers for some help in Spanish, but I did not know the words yet for menstruation or tampon, so this would require a game of charades incorporating pointing to my vagina in public and saying, "Sangre" with my horrid Minnesotan accent. I passed. Option two would be to bleed all day in defeat and explain that is how North Americans do it, or tell people a horse kicked me during the whole breaking process.

I only had two pairs of pants with me for the year. Option two would cut my supply in half. That would mean wearing only my underwear while I washed my other pair for the rest of the year if I gave my blood pants up. That might not be culturally sensitive. So I went with option three, which also was not pretty or ideal. I went into the bathroom and gathered all the toilet paper I could find. This ended up being about one eighth of a roll between all of the stalls.

Toilet paper is never found in bulk in Uruguay, and any toilet paper that is found is not exactly Charmin extra soft. Uruguayan toilet paper is thin to disappearing, dusty almost. Most people carry their own with them at all times. I was still a rookie. I split it in two, and made one tampon out of half and one pad out of the rest. I half laughed and half grimaced as I tried to confidently stride out of the bathroom with my makeshift plug.

Then, about an hour later, I realized I had to go to the bathroom. I laughed out loud as I walked into the bathroom, remembering that I now had no toilet paper left for that, but neither did any women, all day, so I got over it. Plus, pooping had become such a great victory that toilet paper was secondary.

We stayed at the festival for eight hours. I learned that this was just like a rodeo, with riding competitions and live music, but without bleachers or barricades. Horses were blindfolded, mounted, and ridden until the rider was saved from the wild, beautiful beast by two friends on either side. The competition was my church's main fundraiser for the year. Families who lived nearby donated three cows to be slaughtered and sold as concessions. I experienced my first *asado,* where the cows are cooked out in the open. Benches of endless chorizo sausage and rib after rib cooked in the fire. I stepped over a bloody cow shin and hoof on my way to sit.

What a beautiful day. The sun was out, the kids were playing, and my cramps were so bad I wanted to cut my uterus out with a spoon. However, somehow, this was not the worst day of my life. I have learned that if you are going to laugh about it sometime, you might as well laugh in the moment. Somehow, it made watching the Uruguayan cowboys break in the horses all day even more unique and memorable because I sat there for eight hours with a sly smile on my face, knowing that I was in Uruguay with toilet paper stuck up my vagina. Mission work at its best.

March 23

In the U.S., I went so fast because I thought if I stopped I would not be worth anything. I was what I did. I got my worth from the external encouragement that came with success. Well, I have stopped. I am worthless this year. I do not receive the external feedback that I was used to, yet life continues. I am just sad enough, just depressed enough to test it, to challenge God to love me less in my nothingness.

"Look, God! I am not doing anything! I am just taking up space! They do not need me here! In fact, they may be better without me! Hate me! Strike me down!" But I always wake up the next morning, with puffy eyes

from crying. God spares me. Then I realize that no matter how hyperactive or comatose I am, the world changes how it reacts to me but God does not. Hyperactive me gets the illusion of power and control, respect and responsibility. The comatose me is left to keep on living. She gets a bed, food, and a little attention now and then, but basically the right to keep on keeping on. Somehow I feel God letting me know that both versions of me are sacred, beautiful, hurting, human, sinful, quirky creations. God adores me in all my worthlessness and potential. It really doesn't matter. It can't. I figure I will keep testing God all year.

"Look, it is March, and I am still not doing anything!" But I find freedom knowing I will enjoy a beautiful sunset the next night. That sunset will give me the strength to become a co-creator on earth with God, ushering in God's vision of peace and beauty for the world. Everything matters, and nothing matters. May I always dwell in that tension. I can't earn it. I can't deserve it. I never could. That is grace. Life is a gift. We wake up every morning despite what we did yesterday with so much to be thankful for if we choose to have the eyes to see it. Everyday has a new sunset, a new orchestra in the sky to take in, a gift from God. Everyday, grace waits for us to stumble on it.

Soy Yo

You are probably striving to build on identity in your work to protect yourself against nothingness, which is not the right use of your work. All the good that you will do will come not from you but from the fact that you have already allowed yourself, in the obedience of faith, to be used by God's love. Think of this more and gradually you will be free from the need to prove yourself, and you can be more open to the power that will work through you without you knowing it.[9]

THOMAS MERTON

Sometimes, when you don't think you need it but you really need it the most, mercy appears. I had been living in Lascano for three months. The initial high had worn off, but the end was nowhere in sight. In a subversive way, culture shock was eating at my soul. I was in the process of completely reshaping my identity so that productivity and work, success and large numbers of powerful relationships had nothing to do with my worth. I was still starkly the other, the foreigner, the clueless outsider who in no way was a relevant contributor to community. I was sorely disillusioned and numb. My insides were churning and screaming and projectile vomiting. I worked every single moment to suppress the sorrow and confusion of complete solitude.

I had fooled myself into thinking that I was, indeed, fine. I was surviving, in hopes of thriving someday soon. I had told myself so many times that not working was great that my fragmented self almost bought it. But, in hindsight, every day was hard. It was just a matter of how successfully I could lie to myself about how well I was doing at handling the challenges.

Then, totally unexpectedly, on a day I was feeling particularly like a useless North American freeloader, mail came. In that package was a copy of a book titled *My Red Couch: And Other Stories on Seeking a Feminist Faith.* I was published. A year and a half prior, my essay was selected to be amidst twenty essays by young feminist Christians in this compilation project. I had just received my complimentary copy in Uruguay. As if the very pages were holy, I lifted it out of the box and carefully explored it. I found my essay and stared at my name, touching the print to make sure that it was real. My worlds collided. The fragmentation was intense. The Uruguayan Ellie who had no work, no friends, and no identity was holding proof of the United States version of herself, one observing the other from afar. One identity arriving in the mail to the other, reminding my Uruguayan self of the previous version, just months prior, who knew of success, ambition, and articulateness. It was one of the stranger moments of my life, the contrast being stark and noteworthy. In North America, I was a published, accomplished, polished young theologian. In South America, I was a scared, awkward volunteer who considered every day without tears a victory. This was all wrapped up in my heart, fighting for identity space in the same moment.

My North American spirit flooded into me. I was so excited I did not know what to do. I showed my house parents, who graciously showed interest, but could not understand the text. It was encouraging but also ironic. I was still proud. It was still exciting. I put the little jewel in my pocket, the reminder of my other self, and started reading the essays, which I found liberating and dynamic.

Later that day, I ran by a dead, rotting dog on the side of the road, and I ate rabbit for lunch.

November 21
The gospel yesterday was from Matthew 25, Jesus telling the disciples that when they fed the hungry and gave clothes to the naked, when they

loved the least of these, they were loving Jesus. I realized that for the first time in my life, I am the least of these. I had always been the one in power, the one with privilege. I was the one being called on to minister. For the first time in my life, I am begging to be ministered to. I am a foreigner, and each time I have been welcomed, I have seen the face of God. The systems here are not set up for my benefit. When people begin to speak quickly, I am left on the outside. As a foreigner, I have experienced feeling invisible and silenced for the first time in my life. I pray that this year will build up my compassion, so that when I return to the place of power, I will constantly seek out the least of these to offer relief.

I do not live in a hut, but I do live in a place that challenges me to reflect and be vulnerable. I think that is why I came. I had to leave my life in the United States, my life that I was good at and comfortable with, to understand my vulnerability, my country's vulnerability, and our interconnectedness and dependence with the rest of the world and all of creation. Uruguay provides space for reflection and the hospitality of new, uncomfortable ideas. After successfully running the rat race of America for 25 years, I unexpectedly find that Lascano invites me to slow down and dwell in my vulnerability. At times, the new language, new culture, new people, and new ideas are uncomfortable; but I am grateful to be here. I hope that someday, the United States, too, as a nation, will be brave enough to intentionally seek reflection and vulnerability until we realize that the whole world is connected and sacred despite and because of our differences.

> Thus a spirituality marked by the struggle for liberation can lead to an experience of deep darkness, which will require true humility. It is this humility that enables us to continue in the struggle, even when we see little progress, to be faithful even when we experience only darkness, to stay with the people even when we ourselves feel abandoned.[10]
>
> HENRI J. M. NOUWEN

Accompaniment

*For it is in loving, as well as in being loved, that we become
most truly ourselves. No matter what we do, say, accomplish, or
become, it is our capacity to love that ultimately defines us. In the
end, nothing we do or say in this lifetime will matter as much as
the way we have loved one another.*[1]

DAPHNE ROSE KINGMA

October 20

I just got hired to teach gym classes at Ignacio's preschool: ages three
to five. I am super excited, although it will add a grand total of three
hours to my painfully slow workweek. But it is a start. The teachers are
eager to learn, too. This town seems to be thirsting to be inside their bodies
more, in a healthy way. And I really hope God can use my gifts to teach
these kids to love their bodies and be more respectful and less violent to
each other's. I truly think that exercise can be an outlet that is joyful. I am
not saying that because I teach preschool gym that men will instantly stop
beating their wives. But life-giving play and movement is a worthwhile
thing to put time into. They have observed that to be a gift and invited me
to use it, and I am grateful.

Trabajo

As for my father, I never knew whether he believed God was a mathematician but he certainly believed that God could count and that only by picking up on God's rhythms were we able to regain power and beauty.[2]

NORMAN MACLEAN

Many of the kids who came to the program I worked with were not well fed, well educated, or well loved. They were hungry for my attention, affection, encouragement, and safety. Similar to when I was in a city, my job was to listen, love, and motivate children to rise above the oppression and violent nature of the town. The main difference I saw early on was that our town did not have many employment opportunities. Most men either worked in the fields or the rice plant for terribly difficult hours with outrageously low wages. Others lived in towns as far away as the capital and came home twice a month on the weekends to see the kids. Other times, they would meet women there and never come back. The kids I worked with dreamed of being mechanics and hairdressers, farmers and factory workers, moms and maids.

To my embarrassment, my first instinct was to tell them that they could be "more." I don't even know what that means now. Maybe I envisioned them "breaking out" of the small town to learn city life or landing a job that makes more money. I did not get it. Not only will most of these kids need to drop out of school during high school to start making money, but they also do not dream of having the funds to move to Montevideo for college. In fact, the kids only had to, by law, go through the sixth grade, and leaving town after high school was the only educational option. Public colleges have no tuition, but life in bigger towns is more expensive. I realized that I had used money as a mark of how to place value on jobs. I was projecting my interests onto them. Luckily, when I was thinking these things, dreaming my dreams instead of valuing their own, I was not good enough at Spanish to turn those ignorant thoughts into words.

That year, I learned to value jobs that do not make much money. I began to value and see the beauty in farm life and factory work. I began by thinking that my work and much of the work done by the people in Lascano were useless or monotonous, but I learned to value them both. I became excited that the kids wanted to stay in Lascano and make it a more beautiful place. The cycles of oppression will not be broken if they all leave. If the kids have a new vision free of violence, prostitution, and economic exploitation, then we will be blessed to have them dig their heels in and transform Lascano from the inside.

As I began to value their vision of work, I simultaneously began to value the work they were giving to me. After simply being a presence in Lascano for a month, I started to encounter a small sense of call there. It was not at all what I expected it would be. Watching me run and do yoga and knowing that I was a gymnastics coach and athlete back in the United States, Marcelo and Marina asked me to be part of a workshop for teens on peace. My segment was "Looking for Peace Inside Our Bodies." I was also hired at two different schools to be a gym/movement/gymnastics teacher. The teachers eagerly asked me if I would be willing to teach them too, after school. The youth in town who were particularly fascinated with my running wanted me to start a running club. After putting away my "jock" identity after college, the people gently invited me to resurrect it and embrace it. I moved to a town plagued by domestic violence, where the kids are very violent with each other, learning from example. I did not assume that my work would even begin to tackle such huge cycles of oppression, but I do think power resides in movement and exercise, in respecting the strength and beauty and power of our bodies. And I was surprised at how anxious people were to learn how to become more in touch with their bodies.

Looking at my year in hindsight is very humbling. I left for Uruguay with grandiose plans of using my seminary training in the church to transform the community. I was placing more value on being a youth pastor of sorts than being a gym teacher. But that is not what accompaniment is about. By just living there, I let them invite me. I think it is refreshing to think that ministry can look like running and flipping. I was totally wrong when thinking what gifts of mine would be relevant in Lascano. My expectations were replaced by reality, and I walked with the kids of Lascano, not as much as a seminarian, but as an athlete.

So, together, we hung out in Uruguay, trying to hear God's rhythm in our bodies and all around us, and we used that rhythm to move and dance, believing it brought power and beauty into a hurting world. We hoped together that when we dance, God smiles on us. We did good, noble work, and that was enough.

Cama

By becoming poor ourselves, by loving until it hurts, we become more capable of loving more deeply, more beautifully, more wholly.[3]

MOTHER TERESA

Being approachable is an important part of ministry. In my experience, it required a welcoming spirit, a willingness to be available, and a place where I could be found. I only had one place that was truly my own, and that was my bed. Some of my favorite, most precious memories happened while sitting in that bed in my first house. I realized quickly what a huge sacrifice it was for my house family to accept me into their home for a year. Marina told me a few months in that Santiago had the hardest time adjusting. He told his mom, "This is not a hotel. This is our house." I also learned that Marina and Marcelo used to stay in the room I slept in. They moved to Dinorah's smaller room so that I could have more space. Meanwhile, Dinorah's bed was moved so that she shared their old room with me. Her bed was small, like mine. The bed was small, old, creaky, and fairly uncomfortable, but I never took it for granted. That bed will always have a special place in my heart because that, more than any other space during a year filled with my active, brave initiative to get my needs met, is where people approached me and ministered to me.

On countless occasions after a hard day, I would be sitting in bed reading at night when little Ignacio would come into the room in just a white T-shirt and Spiderman underwear to present me with a picture of robots fighting with his name scribbled in the corner. I "oohed" and "ahhed" in gratitude, asked him to explain the robot war to me in detail, and then he casually went back to his room to make me another.

Santiago was by far the toughest to connect with. He was stubborn, standoffish, and very guarded. I rightly predicted early on that eventually he would be my favorite, but the beginning was slow. To try to get him to open up, I played soccer with him whenever he wanted. I would also ask him at night for help on my Spanish pronunciation. We would sit on the couch at night, him looking over my shoulder, at some vocabulary words. I would say it. He would laugh at me. I would laugh at me. Then he would pronounce the word over and over until I got better. Meanwhile, Ignacio would run around the living space coming up with an action for each word to help me remember. But Santi always stayed at my side, quiet, intellectual, and committed to help. He found ownership in my improvement and started showing interest in learning English. But we never stopped laughing, as I never learned how to roll my "Rs."

After months of cautious attempts like these to connect, Santiago unsolicited came straight to my bed after school, without being prodded by anyone, to show me his soccer trading cards and teach me about the big players. I was shocked. He sat on my bed for over an hour talking away, convinced that I would not be a real member of his family until I learned a few things about soccer. I smiled inside and out, marveling at how precious he was.

To connect with Dinorah, I would write paragraphs in Spanish and have her correct them for me. It was a way to make her my teacher and get better at writing, but also breach more difficult subjects with time to think of how to present them. After reading a paragraph about my boyfriend back home, Dinorah came to my bed with her corrections and asked if she could sit. We talked for hours about her boyfriend, who lived in another town. None of her friends understood why she just didn't date someone from Lascano, but she knew it did not need to be easy to be good. I encouraged her and told her we could talk about it anytime she needed. As a "mature beyond her years" thirteen-year-old, she was in an isolated spot. She was not always ready to talk politics and the Church with her parents, but she was usually too grown up to play with her five- and eight-year-old brothers.

Not being from Lascano, she did not quite fit into the social scene. Unlike her friends, she had no interest in staying in Lascano. She wanted to study in Montevideo and even leave Uruguay. Unlike her friends, she had seen and lived in other parts of the world, experienced towns that did not operate like Lascano, and she had the money and intelligence to make these dreams happen. She also had parents who did not let her go out much and a life of a pastor's daughter that had her on the road a lot. That night in my bed, a tangible change of intimacy sparked between us. We conducted the first conversation I remember where I was not in the least conscious of my Spanish flaws. She understood what I was trying to convey to her, which was a message that she was hungry for, so it just did not matter to either of us if my verb tense was conjugated wrong. I told her how beautiful and unique she was, telling her that all the hard work was actually really exciting and cool. I tried to be for her what I already was: someone older than Santiago and younger than her parents who knew what it felt like to be a foreigner in Lascano with an extended family, boyfriend, and dreams located in other places. For the first time, I felt like it might be a positive thing for Dinorah that I lived with her family for a year. She was finally taking me up on my presence in our shared bedroom.

The initial conversation opened our relationship up for further moments of precious interaction. After a trip to see her mother's family in Western Uruguay, which included seeing her boyfriend, Dinorah and I were lying in our respective beds across the room from each other. It was a hot night, and I was exhausted from the six-hour car ride after being even further outside of my comfort zone in a new, even smaller town. As I was drifting off to sleep, I heard Dinorah crying ever so quietly. Unfortunately, my embarrassment in Spanish had trained my first reaction to be staying quiet, but I fought through my first instinct to ignore it and asked her if she wanted to talk. She said yes. So I got out of bed in my underwear and T-shirt (the heat of summer had set in) and joined her in her bed in her underwear and T-shirt.

I trod lightly, sensing immediately the vulnerability of the situation and my role in it. She spoke of how she would not see Fransisco again for over two months, which was an eternity for a thirteen-year-old who feels isolated in her town. I let her cry and scratched her back, trying to offer my awkward Spanish comfort now and again. I asked her questions and let her cry. I invited her to tell me more about Fransisco and watched the excitement of adolescent infatuation pour out of her. After about an hour of this, talking late into the morning, I climbed out of bed and grabbed some stationary, and suggested we both write letters to our far away loves. She nodded eagerly. So she wrote to Fransisco, and I wrote to Dan. I told Dan the situation, tried to paint for him the moment I was experiencing. I told him that I loved him and was counting down the days until he came to visit. But I also told him that it felt good on that night that I was at a place of peace with him being far away, and I was in the position to try to get Dinorah there with me. It made Dan and my love feel worn in and strong. I have no idea what Dinorah wrote to Fransisco. The words were in a different language, coming from a different stage of life, but they came from the same substance as mine.

Two young women who used to live across the world from each other, not knowing the other existed and convinced that they had nothing in common, now shared a bedroom and the angst of long-distance love. It was a beautiful moment of connection with her that I am honored to have been there for. These moments, when someone in Lascano and I breathe easier because I got on a plane, these moments made the whole year worthwhile.

The next day I gave Dinorah a chain made of a piece of paper for every day until she got to see Fransisco again. Each day she could take a piece off the chain and write on it one reason she liked him. On the day she saw him, she could give him all the pieces. She thanked me eighteen times and pleaded with me to keep it our little secret. I smiled as I saw the chain, hanging over her bed, get smaller and smaller, reminding me of the night we wrote letters together in our underwear at three in the morning. I mostly smiled for her, but I knew at the end of her chain, I was a bit closer to seeing Dan, too.

I was constantly trying to connect with my three house siblings while still allowing them to have their own lives and their own space. But it was on that bed that I felt a true first connection with all three. As they entered the one space in all of Uruguay that I could call my own, barriers of age, interest, and hemispheres came down. All that was left was thin space overflowing with precious love. When I think about that bed, I think about sacred space. The bed was a tiny, old, crotchety space, but it was all I had. Space is important, and having our own spaces is part of that. The bed taught me so much because it pointed to the frustration of constantly feeling like an intruder, a guest, a foreigner. The bed was so pivotal because it was the only space where people could approach me. When Ignacio, Santiago, and Dinorah came to sit on my bed, they crossed a barrier. They entered my territory. That trust, that vulnerability is what made having my own space so wonderful. Being approachable is part of ministry, part of being ministered to, part of powerful, authentic, mutual relationship.

Buen Amigo

"But what," badgers a relentless voice, "exactly are you doing out here? What are you accomplishing? What are you getting out of it? And what, oh especially what are you going to do with your life?"

The voice usually stops me. Knocks me down, kicks sand in my
face. But this time, finally, I tell the voice to shut up. It's a stupid
question, what are you going to do with your life. Setting out to
do something with your life is like sitting down to eat a moose.
Nobody ever did anything successfully with their life. Instead, they
did something with their day. Each day.
Sunrise is birth. Sleep is death. Each day is your life.
Let the moose run. Eat some berries.[4]

DOUGLAS WOOD

In orientation, I met Tom, who was also going to Uruguay. Tom
was fresh out of St. Olaf, a social work major, a lovable fatalist with
deep integrity and the will to do the right thing. Very much the
intellectual, he was a strong and intentional communicator with an
easy laugh and a desire to ask big questions.

Orientation leaders told us we would see each other twice a
month, which seemed excessive until we tried refraining from speaking
English in a new culture for fourteen days at a time. The semimonthly
meetings quickly seemed essential to survival. For the first few months,
Tom and I would alternate locations every other week and spend
the weekend together. As we got stronger and more self-sufficient, it
became not even once a month. Regardless of the frequency, I always
thought of our time together as absolutely critical and therapeutic. The
bus ride to Montevideo was five hours, worth every minute.

I do not know what I would have done without him in the
beginning. Our first deep conversation occurred during orientation
in Argentina. The other five had left to meet their fate, and we were
waiting to leave on our journey to Uruguay. We knew we were stuck
with each other, like it or not, so we cautiously asked questions and
told stories until, by the end of a few hours when Tom left to go to
bed, we were relieved and certain that it would be a life-giving match.
We took litmus tests of each other's thoughts on politics, theology,
justice issues, and favorite pizza toppings. We gave backgrounds on
our families and love lives so that we had a context to work from.
We gave first impressions of the other volunteers and even offered
our fears of the next step.

Tom's and my year were very different and very much the same
simultaneously. He was in a sizable city, and I was in the country.
He struggled with bus schedules and homeless men on park benches,
and I struggled with eating cow tongue and not having a coffee shop
to escape to. He worked a lot, and I worked a little. We both saw
hurting kids struggling with violent homes. We both faced the task

of learning a language well enough to become relevant observers in our communities.

Tom was placed in a fascinating community development agency in the heart of a dark, dirty neighborhood working with kids of all ages. He was also placed in a home where he shared a room with two young boys and a house with a little dog that urinated freely inside, including inside of Tom's shoe. Being shaky at Spanish, Tom thought he had misheard, but no, the dog's name was "My Lord" in Spanish. Accompanying My Lord and two sons was a grandma, friend of the family, and husband and wife who made noodles from scratch on the twenty-eighth of every month and were very active in a Pentecostal church.

Tom failed to mention to them that he was struggling with the divinity of Jesus. In that home, it took him months to figure out that he was seriously allergic to the mold on the walls and needed to get his skull X-rayed because of the severity of his four-month-long sinus infection. He learned the ins and outs of the Uruguayan health care system by experience. Eventually, his struggling health got him moved into his own apartment. When I say apartment, I mean a room big enough to fit a bed, desk, dresser, and small stove with a bathroom where Tom could shower, poop, and brush his teeth all at the same time due to close quarters.

Seeing Tom waiting for me at the bus station after my first two weeks in Lascano was relief that I had never felt before. I was completely disillusioned, sick of being weak and mute, hungry and awkward. In a sea of Uruguayan strangers, I met his eyes and was struck by the strength of his smile. I knew someone; someone knew me. His friendship at that moment became one of the biggest comforts of my life. We made it a habit to get ice cream and tell stories for the first few hours we saw each other. It was an English- speaking feast. We vented, processed, laughed, and advocated for each other. The ice cream was an essential piece. We searched high and low for our favorite brand of ice cream and decided on Crufi. Tom bought us two spoons that we brought with us every time we saw each other, knowing there would be laughter and Crufi at some point.

Over Crufi, we came up with the idea of Uruguayan fantasy points. Recognizing that we are socially conditioned to want external reinforcement, we came up with a system of fantasy points for doing things that we do not want to do but knew were good–such as making a bed or initiating a conversation. We updated each other biweekly on how many fantasy points we had given ourselves. The categories changed as our situations did. Some days, I received fantasy points for getting out of bed. Other times, I granted myself points for speaking at a church assembly. One day a few months in, I gave myself three fantasy points for picking up the phone when no one was home, something I used to be scared of, having to answer and communicate in Spanish. It was a fun way to gage improvement, be patient with ourselves, and validate something difficult, such as culture shock, while turning it into a game.

We took trips together to the highest point in the city or the most obscure museum, things we would never muster on our own. We brainstormed ways to send e-mails home in a way that honored the Uruguayans and opened up conversation. We talked of relationships back home, told old college stories, and dabbled in politics, religion, social work, education, and justice, inviting our old selves to join our disillusioned ones at the table and inside of our hearts. We watched World Cup soccer, drank beer, and tried to feel normal for just one afternoon now and again. One weekend when I was struggling in Lascano, Tom brought a bottle of wine on the bus with him. We walked into the cow fields and shared its contents, realizing as the stars became hyper-mobile that we would have to suppress our unintentional tipsiness during dinner, which we did. In fact, the Spanish flowed with lack of inhibition. Tom taught me about bird-watching and introduced me to the band Wilco. He taught me about intentionality, boundary setting, good self-care, and clear communication, saying things such as, "I have really enjoyed talking to you. I am glad you are in Uruguay with me. Just so you know, I think I am going to turn my iPod on and unwind for the rest of the bus ride."

Tom and I thought and felt similarly. It was a gift to be able to spend time with someone with my guard totally down. We decided we would have been friends even if dire circumstances had not absolutely required it. We refueled each other, held each other up, walked with each other in a very tangible way for a year. And we were able to be healthier and happier in our contexts knowing that a Crufi meeting was coming up. We processed deeper being able to do it with each other. We helped advocate for each other. Being in a new culture can be incredibly isolating, and we both had a tough disposition that did not want to complain, even when things got to the point that we desperately needed to get our needs met. We were, for a year, each other's best friend.

My initial instinct to pick a program that would not isolate me came true. Even if I only had one person and even if I was only able to see that one person once in awhile, I was still able to maintain the ability to invoke the spirit of home. We both felt protected and safe with one another, willing to process an unsteady journey full of peaks and valleys, void of middle ground. We were that middle ground for each other. When together, we could rest our muscles and prime our hearts for the next leg of the trip. That was an important part of my year. Tom said it better than I could:

> We see new sunsets this year. Perhaps better put, we feel new sunsets. This one is burning red over the waters and the buildings. We have been talking for hours, sharing our stories and reflections. We span laundry chutes and Titanic videos and the American Games and the role of Jesus. Nothing means everything and everything means nothing. We are experiencing appreciation through deprivation. Our stories include hurt and joy, and our emotions tumble from our mouths. You pick up my wounds and hold them, and I try to do the same for you. Vulnerability is inevitable this year as our comforts and strengths have suddenly disappeared. Thankfully, I have you in this country. With you, I know Crufi and pizza. I arise to the surface and take deep breaths in your presence, temporarily remembering who I am amongst this challenging sea. I can feel whole again. You get on a bus, and I plunge down once more amongst the yelling teachers, violent kids, and consistent insults. Two more weeks and I get to see you again, and I will be refreshed, attempting to make sense of the currents around me.

February 4

Grandpa died on Saturday. I found out today over e-mail. Mom's e-mail made me cry and hurt and feel so far away from home. Everyone was there. He was celebrated and buried next to Grandma. And I missed it. I did not get to say good-bye. I will go home in August looking for him, but I will never see him again. I just want to hug Mom. I sat in the middle of the Internet café and cried harder than I had expected to. I knew this was a risk when I left, and I knew he was proud of me for going. But I feel every single mile between Minnesota and me. Luckily, Tom was checking e-mail right next to me. He let me cry without saying a thing. When I told him what happened, he created a space for me to grieve, to tell stories, as we walked to find ice cream.

Abuelo

And sometimes, when the cry is intense, there emerges a radiance which elsewhere seldom appears; a glow of courage, of love, of insight, of selflessness, of faith. In that radiance we see best what humanity was meant to be… In the valley of suffering, despair and bitterness are brewed. But there also character is made. The valley of suffering is the vale of soul-making.[5]

NICHOLAS WOLTERSTORFF

It took me two weeks to get my family on the phone after I got the e-mail about my grandpa's death. He had died while I was traveling, so communication was complicated. Right after I found out about his death over e-mail, Tom and I had to go further west in Uruguay for a five-day church assembly. Trying to use the phone in this remote place was nearly impossible. When I did talk to my family in the United States, it had been six weeks since our last conversation. One will never totally understand the power of voice until it is taken away. My heart was so anxious to hear about the funeral and make sure that my mom was okay. E-mail was not going to cut it. I was preoccupied with getting my family on the phone. As soon as I heard my parents' voices, I was calmed and comforted. Nothing makes home feel a little bit closer than inflection and character coming through in the spoken word.

My house family never asked me about it, and I never told them. It was a near stranger I met at the church assembly, a woman who worked at a social service agency, who told me she had heard about my grandpa, and offered a single hand on my shoulder as comfort. Her name was Jenny. Born in Australia, she had lived in Argentina since falling in love. She sat for an hour and played with the straggling hair at the nape of my neck after we had a talk about my grandpa dying. It was nice to be touched. The hour that she spent with me asking questions, talking about being far away was a blessing. It seemed so generous to me, I don't know how she knew that I needed it so badly. She told me about missing weddings and funerals, and how very important those big moments are. We also talked about the small moments we missed, such as family dinner or a cup of coffee with an old friend. I realized by the end of the conversation that she maybe needed it, too. These times of connecting so deeply with complete strangers out of necessity and vulnerability, briefly walking with someone I will never see again, having my life changed out of the grace and generosity and compassion shown by someone taking the time to sit with me, these times are the ones that will stay with me forever.

I didn't get through to my parents until well after my conversation with Jenny, but the help she and other strangers offered was so powerful and healing. I missed weddings of five of my closest friends, graduations, births, engagements, and this one funeral. I knew this going into the year, but the reality of that sacrifice set in hard. Jenny knew what it felt like be oceans away from family for the big moments, both good and bad. She knew what it was like to count every wave, every water molecule. While I could not be with my family, she was with me. It helped.

The moment with Jenny on the bench at the church assembly was mirrored, this time in my grief over the loss of Courtney. When Courtney was diagnosed with cancer, Shelly and I bought LIVESTRONG bracelets. The bracelet ended up being quite an unexpected blessing. The fad had not reached Uruguay, so I got asked daily what the English word meant. Almost daily, then, I was able to tell Courtney's story, going into as much detail as my Spanish would allow. This process reminded me that she would not be there when I got home in a year. She could have otherwise slipped easily into the category of friends who lost touch while I was so far away. I grieved quietly and alone, only occasionally sending an e-mail to Shelly to check in with our shared loss. But not a day went by when I did not get to describe her spirit to strangers a hemisphere away. And, somehow, that process turned a bit of my sadness into celebration.

In January, a stunningly mature nine-year-old named Karen did for me what Jenny was able to do when my grandpa died. When she asked about the bracelet, I told her that my very good friend had died of cancer and this bracelet helped raise money to find the cure. She looked up at me and very genuinely said, "That must be hard for you."

Sitting next to her on an old bench, our thighs just barely touching, I instantly teared up. That was the first response I had gotten that created space for me to mourn and be broken. It was the first response that was appropriate, that honored Courtney's life and my loss. I took a deep breath, conscious of the sacred space that I was in and aware that I was being ministered to by an unassuming nine-year-old, and answered simply, "Yes. It has been very hard. Thank you." We sat in silence for a few minutes more before we got called to the next activity and reentered normal space and time. But I will never forget Karen and the simple validation she gave me by making my pain permissible.

When I was leaving for Uruguay, I was acutely aware that I would miss big moments such as weddings and funerals. There is always a fear that disaster will strike while we are far away from the ones we love. I decided to go anyway and found people on the journey who helped me deal with that choice. Both Jenny and Karen showed me a bit about the power of presence, taking time to sit with someone who was hurting. It did not fill the hole made by Grandpa and Courtney's absence, but it did help.

Gracias

God without us will not, as we without God cannot.[6]

SAINT AUGUSTINE

Obviously, Thanksgiving is not celebrated in Uruguay. It was great fun to share my traditions and the ideas behind the American celebration with my community there. I tried to explain Christopher Columbus and Europeans surviving the first winter and how that somehow turned into eating turkey and watching football with family. I was sure they thought I was completely nuts, but somehow they understood that this was the first holiday I was really missing, so Thanksgiving morning my house mom awkwardly approached me, gave me a stiff embrace, and wished me a happy day of thanks.

During orientation, the former volunteers talked about how hard holidays would be. I thought they were talking to other people, because I was tough. I had spent holidays away from family before, and I would be fine. So imagine my surprise when I had to fight back tears at the lunch table on Thanksgiving. Eating oily rice with raisins in it with a family I could barely understand, my mind wandered home to the abundance of laughter, food, and love. I hated admitting that I was human, like the other volunteers, missing home. The original Thanksgiving was probably a celebration of survival and not abundance. That is what my Thanksgiving in Uruguay was about too. I survived.

I was thankful to leave that weekend, take a bus to Montevideo, pick up Tom, and meet the Argentine volunteers in western Uruguay for a retreat. It was still early enough in the year that the English bubbled out of us as we caught up on disastrous, funny, gross, frustrating, and beautiful stories. The sound of my own laughter shocked me, as I had not heard it in a month. We had two cooks in the group who masterfully figured out how to take Uruguayan produce and turn it into the best North American Thanksgiving meal of my life. It was a blessing to speak in English, laugh, cook, and enjoy some familiar food while sharing stories from our families in the United States as well as our new families in South America. I told them about how my family used to drive to Illinois each Thanksgiving to see my aunt. The boys would learn how to shoot with a bow and arrow, and we all had a contest to see who could buy the coolest item for 99 cents or less at Walgreens, the only store open on Thanksgiving. Andrew cried as he relived passing out on his floor, completely horizontal, each year trying to make room for one more helping.

We had become a safe space for each other to miss home and struggle with where we were. We helped each other reflect on what we were thankful for in South America while being honest about what we missed back home. Walking from the common room to our bedrooms that night, stomachs full and cheeks sore from laughing, Andrew looked up at the stars and took a deep breath. A long, slow sigh followed. I realized fully in that moment that we would all have very real challenges, but mine would look completely different than theirs. Living in Buenos Aires where he was dealing with buses, pollution, beggars, and sharing a city with fourteen million other people, he offered, "Man, I have not seen the stars in two months." For the other six, this was a retreat away from the noisy city to the peace and quiet of the Uruguay countryside. For me, it was retreat to easy human interaction, welcomed stimulation.

"That is about all I see," I answered defeated.

We looked at each other, smiled and simultaneously acknowledged, "Different struggles."

November 20

I stood at the window during work and watched the boys in the youth group converse with the construction workers across the street. Our meeting started at 6:30 p.m., but they had come after school to waste time at the church. I could not help but think that, as they stood next to the new building, these boys could be the future of the Church. Marcelo had hooked them, rarely mentioning Jesus, and now they wanted in. There was a safe space created for them, a community of truth and love, and now they were asking questions, seeking, wanting baptism. It is beautiful. The young boys bring energy and enthusiasm, but they do not yet belong. The Waldensians want to help them by giving them food and homework help, but the kids still do not feel welcome to come to church. The interest is there, but the invitation is not. Barriers remain. They long to be a part of something, to feel respected and needed and valuable, part of a community. It kills me that because these kids do not come from a long history of Waldensians, because their skin is darker and their last names are not correct, they remain on the outside. That is not the gospel in action.

Niños

It makes me happy to picture you running around with kids who wonder how your red hair was made.

E-MAIL FROM A FRIEND

A great majority of my time in Uruguay was spent with children. Consequently, my life was often filled with joy. My favorite moments in Lascano included walking past the school to get to work and having ten kids run up to the fence to give me kisses through the wire during recess and ask where I was going. I got showered with hugs, drawings, and kisses from the preschoolers I worked with. Every week they asked when I was coming back. Each day before the after-school program I worked at, I sat outside and took in a few moments of quiet. Every day, two beautiful girls saw me and started running toward me with flowers and kisses ready. They both brought me flowers picked from along the road every day. They taught me that a big part of my job was to accept gifts joyfully as I celebrate the irrational and abundant love of children. I am thankful for children.

Laura and Estrella were best friends. Laura—pronounced as flower without the "F" and an "A" at the end—was eleven. Estrella, which means "star" in Spanish, was ten. They both had to repeat grades a few times, so they were in the third grade together. Laura was the skinniest girl I had ever met. She was over a foot shorter than her friend, Estrella, who had straight, black hair down to the small of her back. Laura had had heart surgery when she was seven months old, and she had another a year after I left. Yet she said she is not scared.

The kids were always the ones that invited me in first, who loved me without boundaries, who saw my differences as reason to be curious instead of reason to exclude me. The little ones were always the ones to call my name out, stretch their arms wide, offer kisses and opportunity for connection. Jesus tells us to be more like children.

In their willingness to love with abandon, without boundaries, irrationally, we do have a lot to learn from them.

When I think back to the children of Lascano, I think of quick love, easy love, irrational love, generous love. They never placed any conditions or expectations, no reservations or hesitation. The love of the children was abundant and constant. Jesus was right: we should strive to make our faith look more like the love of children.

December 14

Ignacio wanted to go running with me today. I let him, and man is he tough! He is five-years-old, and made it really far! When we got back, we wrestled. For no reason at all, he grabbed a comb and started combing my hair, turning the living area into a pretend barbershop. I instantly turned into a "zombie" and soaked up the gentle attention.

Maté

The miracle is not to walk on water, the miracle is to walk on the green earth dwelling deeply in the present moment, and feeling truly alive.[7]

THICH NHAT HANH

Maté is a staple in Uruguay. It is a tea that everyone drinks communally and constantly, partially because it is cheap and partially because in a poor country, hunger suppressants are key. Outside the gas stations in the U.S., we have machines to put air in our tires. In Uruguay, we had machines of hot water to refill maté thermoses. This was serious business. I told Dan before he came that everyone in Uruguay drank maté, and he thought that I meant like everyone in the United States drinks coffee or soda pop. He was stunned at my definition of everyone. As we walked down the streets of Montevideo, he verbalized his surprise that one in every two people were enjoying maté as they walked down the street.

A maté is actually a gourd, made out of leather or wood usually. They vary in size, shape, and color; but most somehow resemble an opened softball covered in dark leather. No tea bag for Uruguayans. They take yerba leaves, which look like green tea leaves, place them directly in the maté, and then pour hot water over a section of the leaves, trying to keep some of the tea leaves fresh for later. The water, now infused with yerba flavor, is sipped from a metal straw with tiny holes on the bottom to filter the water from the leaves. Rookies have compared the bitter taste to things like dirt and grass. Such definitions normally exude from a face that is reacting to the temperature of the water and the foreign taste.

In Argentina, some people take their maté dulce, with sugar. In Uruguay, we are purists. The matés are also bigger, and the yerba leaves smaller. The further East we go, the less the people are messing around. I first needed to get used to the temperature, as I did not drink so much as coffee in the United States. In Uruguay, even in the summer, the hotter the water the better. If the water was not hot enough, some of the yerba could sneak up through the tiny holes in the metal straw and ruin the sip. As soon as I adjusted to the scalding nature, I was severely emotionally attached to the taste. I loved what it stood for: community, conversation, communion. The person with the maté is in charge of filling it with water transported from a kettle on the stove or fireplace to a thermos. Then the thermos possessor passed the maté around the circle as people drink from it one by one, as the others anxiously awaited their turn. Maté is used as breakfast, with snacks, at meetings—at the center of a leisurely afternoon conversation as well as by individuals throughout the day.

Maté is a hunger suppressant and contains what is called mateine, similar to caffeine without the addictive side effects. I did not believe that until I came home. Scaling back from two thermoses a day to maybe one a week, I did not, indeed, go through any physical withdrawal. Emotional withdrawal was a different story. If I drank too much maté early in the year, I would get stomach rot, shaking hands, and the inability to fall asleep at night. It began as a bridge, a way I could be invited into the culture and show that I was willing to assimilate and honor what the people honored.

"She drinks maté?" I would hear strangers ask my host family with a surprised yet impressed tone as I sipped without wincing.

Early on, it was a conversation starter. "You like maté? Do they have that in the United States? Did you ever drink it there?" Sometimes, when language was a barrier, it acted as the one thing that connected me to what was going on. Even if I could not participate verbally, I could accept the maté, drink from it, and pass it back. In that way, I felt like a real person, a part of the community.

If one is passed the maté and says, "Thank you," it actually means, "No thank you, I have had enough." I had a hard time accepting the maté without giving thanks, but it was a good exercise for me. Often, my house mom walked into another room altogether to hand me the maté when it was my turn; and I graciously and silently stopped whatever I was doing to be reminded that nothing I was doing could be more important at that moment than building community and being present. Plus, it just tastes really good.

Early in the year, I was caught crying a bit in my shared bedroom, against my best efforts. I generally don't like people to know that I am human. Marina came and sat on my bed with me. After a few comforting words in Spanish, she concluded with, "And there is maté." I joined the family downstairs, and the warm maté was sustaining and comforting.

Sharing maté was a powerful, spiritual experience for me. It was countercultural from the culture I knew. Uruguayan people knew no higher priority than to sit with each other, converse, and pass the maté. In the circle, communion happened. Dreams, gossip, laughter, and tea were shared. The maté made no distinctions. Everyone was welcome; everyone received. It filled us up and sustained us, literally and figuratively. Taking in the earthy taste, the warmth, the hospitality, pulling the tea into me that was plentiful and generously passed, there was a sense of being profoundly present in the moment, radically dwelling on the green earth, and feeling totally alive.

In my pre-Uruguayan life, I never drank tea because I did not have the time. I did not live slowly enough to heat water and fill myself with anything that had to be sipped delicately as opposed to gulped functionally. Maté taught me about living slowly enough to experience the fullness of the moment, to connect with the earth beneath me, and to commune with the people around me. After sharing maté with a complete stranger, something changes. You experience a special feeling of connection afterward. You create space for sharing each other's reality. Maté levels us as equals, invites conversation, and capitalizes on each moment we are given.

The people there describe maté as the opposite of television. If you are with other people, it is a time to converse; if you are alone, it is a time to think. With maté, they would say, there is no young or old, no man or woman, no rich or poor. If someone comes to your door, no matter who it is, you are to say, "Hello," and, "Would you like maté?" It welcomes, connects, offers hospitality and good wishes. It invites strangers in and evaporates previous barriers. If we in the U.S. still hold on to the idea of going over to a neighbor's house for a cup of sugar, they would give a neighbor yerba without a second thought. People drink it not to drink, but to take in conversation. People drink it to share love, to share life, and to take the time to give thanks at least once every day.

Eventually, after being the one predictable and constant part of my year, I could not live without it. Even if I was just among the other six North Americans, where maté would not normally be our default, craving and instinct would soon kick in. Someone would always put water on for maté, connecting us, soothing us, an ever-present companion.

I was gifted three different maté gourds at the end of the year to bring back because it truly embodies the culture. If a single object can symbolize the country, it is this. It may never flourish in the United States, however. My first year back, I gave a lot of talks about Uruguay, and sometimes I would bring maté to share. People often passed because of fear of germs, which was disappointing to me. It seemed paranoid and sterile. Others would want to try it, excited that it was a hunger suppressant, thinking of losing weight instead of realizing that the people in Uruguay did not have enough to eat. But after one taste, grand plans of dieting would fall by the wayside. The best I got was usually a kind smile and nod, and then a return to bottled spring water or Diet Coke. When I drink maté in the United States, then, it is usually by myself, which is even more than "just not the same." It is completely missing the point. Drinking maté invokes lovely memories and warms my innards, but the magic of the spirit that dwells where two or more are gathered and bonded by the passing of maté simply is not present. Second to the people, I miss maté the most.

Escribiendo

Writing became a door to contemplation and a channel for grief.[8]

HEIDI NEUMARK

January 23

Sometimes people get uncomfortable when I tell them that I am writing a book about my year in Uruguay, but it is the easiest way to explain why I am writing all the time. A cousin of my house family asked me at lunch, "So you are a writer?" Choosing the path of least resistance since it was a bad Spanish day, I just agreed—although my instinct was to quickly deny it. So after I said yes, I contemplated it awhile, trying the new occupation on for size. I am here to see things, to make connections. I just always thought it would be for my own personal growth, but maybe it is to share. I really don't think that I am a writer, but maybe I am someone who writes, a small part of who I am.

October 6

    Sometimes I wonder if I write too much. I feel like Tom Hanks in Castaway, *when he befriends the volleyball. I write to an inanimate object in desperate need of companionship, talking and processing. It is my escape. But then again, I am doing my fair share of seeing and hearing, and I do not want to lose any of it. I am increasingly getting the sense that it is my job to observe and then take this place back home, maybe by writing, maybe by speaking. Here, for the first time in my life, God has called me to finally sit still, quiet my heart, to see, to think, to write, to be. Or maybe it is just the first time that I listened. Or maybe it is just the first time that I obeyed, not having much of an option. It is different, but it is wonderful. I have lived twenty-five years as fast and full as possible. Now, it is as if it is all coming out of me, and I am finally trusting the value of a reflective and contemplative life. I get continued encouragement from home to send more e-mails and to write a book when I return. As "useless" as I feel here (I am actually getting comfortable with my role as relevant observer and deep down know that I am only useless in the eyes of North American society), I feel very powerful in the United States. I must continue to recognize the power of my words, choose them carefully, and process through e-mail with integrity. The response back home has given me enough sense of vocation here that I am energized and hopeful, not as lonely and not wishing for a life of comfort back home. Well, in time, but not now.*

    I am getting the sense to be myself with my words and write with an audience not because I am brilliant. I am not. Not because I am going through something unique and hard and better than life in the United States—wrong. This is not deeper or more filled with integrity—not at all; my life here is clumsy and small. And I am not the only person to ever travel to Uruguay. But I think I am being called to use my voice because I have one and because an appalling apathy and silence engulfs good people here. I may not be saying anything new or exciting, but I am saying something. Someone just might be listening, someone also inspired to speak, empowered to find a voice. Together, our community of goodness may just do something small and beautiful in the world.

December 23

    Mary is not Jesus, but she was a woman who knew the pain of being rejected, judged, despised, forgotten and pushed aside. She gave birth in a barn, had a son who caused trouble, watched that son be tortured and killed. Mary must have a word of hope and solidarity for the women of Lascano.

Navidad

Christmas is about God with arms.[9]

HEIDI NEUMARK

Everyone said that Christmas would be hard. It was a little hard. A better word to describe it would be unique. It was quiet, calm, and quite uneventful compared to Christmases of my past. Rural Uruguay builds up to Christmas in a quite limited manner. I did not bake cookies, go shopping, listen to carols, or decorate a tree. Although I missed the music, time with family, and even the snow, I did not miss the hectic and over-secular rush before Christmas.

My Christmas celebration started on December 21, when I rode thirty minutes through the cow fields with Marcelo to a church service. In pure, rural Uruguayan style, the worship started over an hour late. The service featured two baptisms, only one of which the pastor knew about beforehand. I was following the homily in Spanish until a large roach fell from the ceiling and attached stubbornly to my hair. That distracted me momentarily. I eventually regained composure and enjoyed the rest of the service. I also appreciated the sweet bread and homemade wine we shared afterwards.

Christmas Eve in my family in the United States is a day full of events, food, family, and church. In comparison, my Christmas Eve in Uruguay was very quiet and lonely. I went for a run, started a novel, received some lovely phone calls from the U.S., and took a long walk into the farm fields. As I sat with the cows, I felt lonely knowing what I was missing at home, but not sad. I could not help but think that the actual birth of Jesus was probably like this—quite ordinarily warm, simple, and quiet. I knew this holy day might just prove to be the only Christmas I spend in a T-shirt hanging out with farm animals in South America, so I was patient with my loneliness, not letting it escalate to despair, distracted by the novelty.

I went to a Catholic mass that evening by myself. Although I was too tired to retain all of the Spanish, the rhythm was familiar from my childhood, which was comforting. It was nice to look around in the community of 150 to see faces I recognized from living there for a few months. At one point in the mass, I was disturbed. Two Lascano kids with beautiful dark hair, skin, and eyes carried a manger to the front. The priest unveiled a strikingly white baby Jesus with a full head of blonde hair. The congregation approached the figure after mass to kiss one of its toes. I felt blessed to receive communion, but I skipped out on the toe kiss, extremely aware of my own blonde hair among the beautiful black locks of most gathered. Why is baby Jesus blonde, here in South America?

At half past eleven that night we sat down to eat the famous rice-eggs-potato combo salad and "pig." I love that we just called what we were eating what it was. We didn't eat steak; we ate cow. For Christmas, we had pig. At midnight, we wished each other a *Feliz Navidad* as we rushed outside to watch the fireworks. The show was short, but magical all the same. Watching Ignacio full of delight–mixed with a healthy dose of fear–at the nearness and power of the fireworks proved enjoyable. Returning to the house, Papa Noel had visited. Each family member had one package to open. Santi and Ignacio each got a flashlight and small toy car. Dinorah got a Ché T-shirt, and I was gifted my own maté gourd and thermos so I could drink maté when I returned home. I almost started to cry.

Christmas Day was also shockingly quiet. I went for a run, finished the 700-page novel I had started the day before, took another walk, and helped set up the church for the service, which started only twenty minutes late. Instead of the normal crowd of about ten people, we had seventy show up for Christmas. The celebration consisted of a modern-day, Lascano version of "the least of these" acted out by the kids in the youth group. Then we were treated to half an hour of singing. For three minutes, it felt like Christmas when the choir sang "Silent Night" in Spanish. I realized that the hope and joy Jesus brought into the world by becoming flesh is truly universal. I was overwhelmed during those three minutes. I saw light and love birthed and shared in the celebration in a little town in Uruguay. What a gift!

Novio

Oh, the comfort,
The inexpressible comfort of feeling safe with a person,
Having neither to weigh thoughts nor measure words,
But pouring them all out,

Just as they are
Chaff and grain together,
Certain that a faithful hand will take and sift them,
Keep what is worth keeping,
And with a breath of kindness blow the rest away.[10]

DINAH MARIA MULOCK CRAIK

At the end of January, my boyfriend Dan came to see me for ten days. My heart went through quite a transition. I had survived for months without speaking in English, receiving hugs, or being able to love or be loved in a deep, familiar way. He showered me with affection, laughter, active listening, and companionship. He put me back together with his kisses. The first afternoon was spent sharing stories and basking in the reality of each other's presence. He brought me cards and gifts from home to open. My brother had sent pictures from a whole roll of film he had used at Christmas. As I flipped through them, I started crying out of longing, loneliness, and the stark contrast between my reality and what I sacrificed by leaving the people I love. Dan held me—my body and my burdens—for those ten days. My load felt lighter. He reminded me that I was beautiful, intelligent, strong, courageous, and worthy. In a moment I went from survival to abundance.

He pampered me, and I let myself be pampered with good wine, fancy food, quaint hotels, and little adventures. I had a hand to hold on the train. I had someone to talk to over meals. It was revolutionary. This was the first time in my life I let myself need someone. Without a shadow of a doubt, I needed Dan. I showed him Buenos Aires, Montevideo, the ocean, and Lascano. He met all my North American friends, and we talked about the future. Those ten days stand apart from every other day in the year. It was, as best as I can describe it, a dream, exactly the respite I needed halfway through the year to get me through.

It was interesting to have a visitor halfway through my year. I was spending time in South America with someone who was even more foreign to the situation than I. I had to take control, show him my new home, and do all the speaking, since his bilingual capabilities (limited Norwegian) would get us nowhere. I felt empowered when he relied on me to order food at a restaurant or tell him background information that I had acquired in my time there. In contrast to him, I was finally able to give myself some credit for how far I had come since September. Since he had even fresher eyes than I did, I asked him to tell me what "struck" him, in order to re-spark that critical lens in me. And, when I finally came home after the year, it was helpful to have someone in my life who had at least seen where I had been and had gotten a taste for what I experienced.

The act of devotion, flying to South America to see me, transformed our relationship. One of Dan's most beautiful strengths is his ability to accompany, to be my companion. That trip embodied and personified companionship. Other people said they would call, but he actually picked up the phone, sometimes multiple times a week, and asked me how I was doing. Other people said they would come to see me, but he actually showed up. That act made all of the difference.

He continued to "accompany" me the entire year, even after he had to physically return to the U.S. Beyond the ten days we were able to reconnect in person, his consistent support over the year held me up. Staying so deeply connected to someone back home gave me roots and courage. He called more often than he said he would. He wrote letters and e-mails, sent packages, and never let me feel forgotten. A month before his visit, I got a videotape he had made with all my friends and family wishing me Merry Christmas—the United States saturating my Uruguayan living room. We read the same books at the same time and talked about them on the phone. We prayed at the same time every day to try to feel more connected. He spent time with my friends and family over the year so he could relate to me how they were doing. He held my pain, told me he loved me, and most of all waited for me to get back. I have never known such commitment. It was so painfully difficult to be away from him for a year, but in that year, we taught each other so much, transcending time and distance.

> I go out into the world and trudge through the gravel on
>   my knees, wilting
> You call me back gently, offering warm arms and soft
>   carpet
> In the first mindful inhale, we begin to put me back
>   together
>
> ELLIE ROSCHER

June 10

I have begun to trust in what will come if I just put myself in a position of possibility with an open heart. Without much thought, I went to the plaza in the middle of town a little early to wait for Tom to arrive from Montevideo. I had amazing conversations. Four of my English students were waiting for the bus, too. One was going to Chuy to see his dad, who lives there. Two others were waiting for their dads to come home from two-week stints in the capital. The fourth was going to the next town to shop. They were full of questions, so excited to see me outside of the classroom. Moments like that cannot be created, but living through them forms us.

Estranjeros

I swear never to be silent whenever and wherever human lives endure suffering and humiliation. We must always take sides. Neutrality helps the oppressor, never the victim. Silence encourages the tormentor, never the tormented. Sometimes we must interfere when human lives are endangered. When human dignity is in jeopardy, that place, at that moment, must become the center of the universe.[11]

ELIE WIESEL

Outsiders always find each other. It took a few months, but I finally found some outsiders to fit in with. Michael and Simon were high school exchange students from Europe. They wanted to practice their English, which we all spoke better than Spanish, and I was ready for some friends. I laughed as I walked down the street with Simon, who wore a long black cape, knee-length boots, and studded leather jewelry—and let his fingernails grow to triangle-like points; and with Michael who was more than a foot taller and seven years younger than I. Under other circumstances, we would have never seen each other as peers, as friends, but in Lascano, somehow it worked. We were the three foreigners in a town that did not like foreigners, so we gravitated to each other in our otherness. They liked to rent movies in English and have me try to stump them with obscure vocabulary. They were no replacements for my friends back home, but they offered me a very special companionship.

In the U.S. I had never been an outsider before in any capacity. I was well off, white, accomplished, well-liked... I never had to seek out friends or spend time with people by default. Socially, I did not normally mingle much with people who dressed counterculturally, as did Simon, or people much younger, like Michael. Because I was a foreigner for the first time in my life, I was forced to either be lonely or find other fringe factors.

Recognizing myself as an outsider helped me connect with other outsiders. We are all more alike than we are different, but somehow misfits feel more comfortable connecting to other misfits. Having this opportunity—out of necessity—of connecting with people whom society skips over, plus being one myself, radically revised my vision of life. Making friends with Michael and Simon helped open my eyes to see people on the outside when I was on the inside, which became important when I returned to my position of privilege and power in the U.S.

Identifying myself as an outsider with Michael and Simon helped me to actively seek out other outsiders. For instance, I made friends with a boy who was a beggar in Montevideo. One night, three of us ate dinner outside. These little boys, probably around eight years old, asked for money. We ended up not giving them money, but we did talk to them for about thirty minutes. One boy in particular took a liking to us. The next night, I was walking in the same neighborhood and saw the same boy. He remembered me, and we approached each other like friends. He did not ask me for money, but just wanted to talk. A few weeks later, I saw him during the day with his family on the street. I called to him, and he came to shake my hand. His family looked healthy and happy, which was a surprise to me, in connection to a boy asking for change. Getting beyond the money proved a powerful experience. He saw me as more than a rich tourist, and I saw him as more than a beggar. Those interactions gave me courage to strike up conversations with people such as cab drivers and street performers. More often than not, I found that they appreciated the human interaction. Almost always, their life stories were fascinating. We can build intimacy with anyone we see as a fellow human being. The conversation is just more interesting if everyone is invited to the table.

November 23

If I spend the whole year yearning for home, I will never be present here. The initial shock is over. The story has a few chapters written. The journey is underway. It is time to settle in. I am home. It is time to embrace Christ's attitude and start fresh in Uruguay—ready to embrace it and be present here. I want to learn and act and give and live. It is time to dig my heels in so that I can accompany, walk with, be joyful, observe, see God who is already here, to listen and love. This year is about receiving, not giving. I am helpless, and I need to receive help. It is a gift to the giver and receiver.

Compamento

Since you cannot see into the future, you simply proceed to put one stone on top of another, and another on top of that. If the stones get knocked down, you begin again, because if you don't nothing will get built.[12]

MARY-WYNNE ASHFORD

I was fortunate enough to spend the month of January as a camp counselor in Palmares on the eastern coast of Uruguay. The only expectations I had of what camp could be like came from my many Lutheran friends who have a plethora of memories from summers by lakes, or mountains if they are lucky, playing with kids and sleeping in bunks. It was an amazing month of my life filled with energy, learning and love accompanied so beautifully by the sounds of the ocean. My workday lasted from 8 a.m. to 1 the next morning on a normal day. I got up each morning to run on the beach and center myself before the day began. I spent the entire month wet from either sweat, salt water, or well water, wearing flip flops—outside, dirty, exhausted, and happy. I took naps in the shade with ants crawling on me. I made campfires and watched the sun set over the ocean. I had a child on each arm every minute of every day. I washed my clothes in a bucket once a week and chopped wood to heat the water and cook the food. A million little moments took up residence in my heart forever. All put together they transformed me. I want to share a few quick glimpses.

Leaving Lascano for the first camp, all the kids arrived at the church at 7 a.m. We loaded them into the back of a huge truck, where they sat with the food and supplies on the two-hour drive to our oceanside camp. I felt unsettled as I waved good-bye to them, climbed into the pastor's car, and got out on the other end of the trip without earth caked in my hair, like it had from riding in the back of the truck. Each week the truck would show up with a new group of kids from Lascano, so dirty with road in their hair and excited to start the week. It gave me renewed energy to carry on as we loaded the tired and emotional group from the week before to head back home. After the last camp was over, I was able to ride back with the kids in the truck, which will always be one of my favorite memories. It was a small, but powerful, way for me to connect with them as the gravel roads covered us all together. Two girls, Luciana and Carina, cried almost the whole way back, sad that the experience was over and overwhelmed by what had happened. If I had been fluent in Spanish, I might have tried to fix the situation and talk to them until they clamed down. But instead, I think I did the better thing just sitting between them, handing them toilet paper to blow their noses, and scratching their backs. They were heading back to hard lives in Lascano after a week of ocean and playing and laughter. They probably did not leave Lascano again until camp the next year.

In the third camp, one of the campers was twelve-year-old Sergio. He was just starting to care about his looks. Some pretty cute girls attended this session of camp. Every time we got wet–whether it was the two trips a day to the ocean, the bucket showers, or games involving drenching them–Sergio would ask me if he could use my comb to run through his mid-ear length hair. Eventually, I just started anticipating and handed it to him when his hair was wet. By the end of the week, I was carrying the comb on me. On the last day as I was loading them into the back of the truck, I handed him my pink, fifty-cent comb and told him I wanted him to have it and think of me and the camp when he combed his hair. He was so excited it surprised me. Two tears escaped his big brown eyes. That was more than enough thanks for me.

One camp activity involved having a secret friend. We would draw names and write notes to the friend all week to see if they could guess who we were. Every week, several of the kids asked me for help writing their notes. I thought at first that they were being lazy or did not think they were creative enough to do it. It finally dawned on me that they did not know how to write. They were not asking me just for ideas. They gave me the paper and pen and asked me to actually write it for them. Some said it was to disguise the handwriting, but the leaders confirmed my suspicion. Several kids had not yet learned to read and write. They were being held in the sixth grade, until, at age fifteen, they were able to stop attending school and go work in the fields. It helped me be more patient with the constant requests for my energy. They simply were avoiding embarrassment.

My days with the kids were a mix of playing capture the flag in the sand; being asked as an English speaker for every word to every song ever performed by Green Day, the Black Eyed Peas, and Red Hot Chili Peppers; playing soccer; drinking maté; holding a rope in the ocean so that they knew how far they could swim; and just hanging out.

Most of my lessons were learned in long, subtle, sweeping movements barely recognizable to me. Sometimes, throughout the year, intense moments of learning grasped me. A comment or an event would stop me in my tracks– a welcomed interruption that taught quickly enough to have me on my heels. One of those moments happened at camp. Without realizing it, I was always judging the pastor and his wife for how they did things. I thought they did not work hard, were not organized, did not value punctuality and quick results. That wore on me, as it definitely conflicted with *my* style. I imagine they judged me right back for how I went about my life and work. One day, Marcelo had given me a task in a complicated game that took much setting up and supervision. I went straight away and did it. About an hour later, long after we were supposed to start, Marcelo asked me if I had completed my task. I just said, "Yes," but what I was thinking was, "Of course, an hour ago."

He had a very telling and interesting answer. He looked at me and smiled, "Why did I even need to ask? You are American efficiency." He saw it in me all year because I embody it. It instantly made me realize that I had been placing judgment on simple, cultural differences. I saw him as lazy and inefficient, which I placed a negative value on. He just saw me as different, North American. That interruption changed the rest of the year. I was able to see his differences as gifts. He embodied Uruguay. Learning that lesson made me thank God that I had not been given any power so it had been impossible for me to project my ideals on people who were perfectly happy not sticking to a schedule.

The most intense camp was with the kids who were between fourteen and sixteen. The boys outnumbered the girls by a lot. The energy level was always bordering on uncontrollable. It was the most challenging camp, but also my favorite. The most challenging part was being with boys who were experimenting with their sexuality. I was watched every minute of every day, and they often made me feel dirty doing the most menial tasks, such as spitting out toothpaste after brushing my teeth. I dreaded swimming time, when I was made to stand still in the water in my suit, holding the safety rope while the boys approached me with any number of flirting tactics: splashing, talking, showing off, telling me that they loved me. Yet these same boys who were my biggest challenge at the beach and in Lascano loved playing in the sand and getting letters from their secret friends. Despite my treating them as adults, they were still kids. Seeing the little kid side of them come through without reservation helped me have patience and understanding in our dealings during camp and for the rest of the year after we had all returned to Lascano. All the challenges of the camp were worth it because the intense nature of the week had assisted us in building relationships with each other.

One day, the leader rallied the kids together and told them that we needed to do some physical labor for upkeep of the campgrounds. The same kids who sometimes rolled their eyes at games they ended up loving jumped at the opportunity to feel useful and give back. I was shocked at how excited and willing to help they were. I was put on a team with Jairo and Walter, two fifteen-year-olds who at times had really given me trouble back in Lascano. While others painted or hammered some nails, we used tiny shovels to dig a knee-deep trench that stretched for about fifty yards so the water from the bathrooms would stop backing up. Awesome. We were building a poop river.

I watched in utter amazement as these two guys picked up their tools and went to town. These were farm kids in their element. They were amazingly strong and tough. They never complained and rarely rested. Watching them work with an efficiency that bordered on beauty, I had never felt so much like a weak, rich, city girl in my life. My hands, once tough from gymnastics, blistered immediately. My arms were sore for days afterward. I loved being in a place where we cut our own wood to heat a fire to cook our food or take a warm shower, a place where we dug tunnels when asked to. Jairo, Walter, and I will never be the same again. I gained so much respect for them watching them in their element. As we rejoined the group, having completed the task side-by-side, filthy and blistered but with a huge sense of accomplishment, I think they had gained a little respect for me right back. I had, after all, kept up.

When it was time for the kids of that camp to climb back onto the truck and head for home, these two boys who had come off as the toughest and strongest broke down crying. I sat with Walter, one of the fifteen-year-olds who could not read yet loved manual labor. I hugged him from behind. He did not move to embrace me, but he did not push me away. He sunk his weight into my arms and did not hide his shaking shoulders from me. I could feel the weight of his emotions flow into me. He was letting me hold part of his load.

He was returning to a dirty town where his dad was not around. There he shared a tiny house with six siblings, worked hard in the fields—making his hands look like those of a weathered adult—and received no respect from his peers. We had offered him a week of retreat at the ocean and a space where he felt seen and appreciated. He would have to wait until the following year to leave Lascano again. As that reality set in for me, my heart broke for him. Visions of leaving him for good in July rushed into my head. As the truck drove away, I could still see tears falling under his sunglasses down his stoic face. My heart was heavy, and my body was exhausted, but I knew that I could return to the ocean to be put back together. Walter could not.

On my last night, I left the kids in the bunks with the other leaders and enjoyed a night sleeping on the beach. It was peaceful as the waves reminded me all night long that I am adored, that it will be okay. It was a homage, of sorts, to the ocean for being my refuge. A few of the stars snuck through the clouds, and the waves were amazing. I was the only one on the beach. God felt very close and very far all at once. I felt full. I felt at peace. I woke early to watch the sunrise. As I was taking it all in, I felt a fierce movement in my midsection. There was no time. I sprung from my sleeping bag and made it to some wild grass where the sand begins to turn to land. There before all of nature, I emptied out the entire contents of my large intestine in record time. By this point, I should have been prepared for anything at anytime, but I had not thought to bring toilet paper with me. I looked around at the shrubbery and pictured odd South American rashes spreading on my backside. I realized I had only one option. I left my pajamas at my sleeping bag and sprinted into the ocean. It was freezing and completely exhilarating, and practical as well. I looked around, praying the early fishermen decided to sleep in, and took in the fact that I was skinny dipping in the ocean by myself in Uruguay at sunrise. I laughed out loud and thought, "Oh, if the ELCA could see their missionary now."

It was so powerful to get these kids out of Lascano for a week. It was powerful for me to be gone for a month. It was an intense immersion experience, with the ocean calling my name during breaks to calm me and offer me a rejuvenating solitude. When the kids were napping, I often stole away for an hour-long walk on the beach. I felt alive and strong, energized and empowered. Uninhibited, I stretched my arms out, turned my face to the sky, and filled my soul with fresh air. Not a single person in the entire world knew where I was or what I was doing, but I was not alone. Those moments were the purest worship for me. My joy, my identity was not tied to anyone or anything. It was just God and I in creation smiling at each other. On the beach during my walks, I came to know true grace, peace, mercy, life, and love. It was an important place for the kids, too. They got away from Lascano, a town that is not aesthetically pleasing in the least, and played in the waves. I saw them become rejuvenated, empowered by the beauty and the fresh wind. No matter what our context is, retreating in a new reality can be excellent therapy. Sharing the beauty and power of the ocean with the kids of Lascano was transformative for us all.

So far away from phones or mailmen, I prepared myself to be cut off completely from my life in the United States for the month. To my surprise, the love of my friends and family were more persistent than I imagined. As each load of children came for a new week of camp, one of the adults would approach me with Christmas cards and packages that had arrived back in Lascano for me. It was overwhelming to be able to connect and feel the love and support from home even on a remote bunk bed by the ocean in South America.

After a month barefoot in the sand playing with the kids of Uruguay, returning to my house in Lascano proved interesting. I had not missed the constant noise of Cartoon Network at all. Nor had I missed feeling like a nuisance in a strange home. It was nice, however, to have dry floors. I was immediately struck with feelings of isolation again, going from being overstimulated to under. Going from having a whole beach to myself to sharing a home with a family who may or may not want me. I had to remember to breathe once again, like that first night I arrived. But I was different, changed, by the children and the waves.

December 9

I crawled onto Marcelo and Marina's bed to join Ignacio. I used the opportunity to be a presence to him and work on my Spanish using the "Scooby-Doo" voiceovers as my teachers. During the commercials, I gave Ignacio airplane rides as he bubbled over with joyful giggles. During the show he would minister to me without knowing it, first putting his little leg on my leg, then using my shins as the back of his chair and finally laying right on top of me while I put my arm around him until it was exactly where he wanted it. It was startlingly precious, a sacred moment shared.

Gimnasia

I do not believe the wicked always win. I believe our despair is a lie we are telling ourselves… [W]ith all of us working where we see work to be done, the world will change. And we have to do it by showing up places, our bodies in places—turn off the *** computers, leave the Web and the Net—and show up, our bodies at meetings and demos and rallies and leafleting corners… You exist…You specifically exist… Now get busy.[13]

TONY KUSHNER

Every Tuesday and Thursday from 7 to 8 p.m. was Ladies Hour at the gym in Lascano. When I say gym, I mean an open space about as big as a basketball court. The average age of participants, including my twenty-five years, was about sixty. We spent a good part of the hour walking in a circle, mixing in some jogging, sit-ups, and leg raises. Some days we used pop bottles with water in them for arm weights, and we laid out dirty mattresses on the gym floor for cushions when we did our abs. On step aerobics days, we pulled from the closet little boxes that had been handmade from two-by-fours. The other ladies actually stopped and watched me when it was time to stretch. I only broke a sweat when it was really hot. So why did I keep showing up? I went to walk with the ladies, to rub elbows with the people in my town, to build relationships. But I never expected quite so much to come from Ladies Hour.

One woman who came to exercise found out I was offering English lessons. Her son and his two friends became my favorite students. She was dumbstruck when I told her that the classes were free. On a side note, because of how far I lived from my director and how money works in Uruguay, I received my stipend in bills worth 1,000 pesos, each equivalent to about forty dollars. I always caused quite a scene when I needed to break my bills at these small businesses. When I entered the phone company building to wish my dad a happy birthday, I cowered as I approached the desk with my 1,000 pesos in hand. Then I saw that the employee was my new friend from Ladies Hour. We chatted as she made change, never mentioning or hinting at the inconvenience.

In addition, the teacher of Ladies Hour happened to be the gym teacher at the high school. Finding out about my background, he begged me to come lead a gymnastics unit with his students. These may seem like little things, but they were victories for me, and beautiful examples that relationships do matter.

My favorite relationships in Uruguay were the unexpected ones that came from being part of a community for a substantial period of time. Another example involved the man who worked at the Internet café. On my return to Lascano after ten weeks away, he welcomed me with a friendly, "You have returned! I thought maybe you went back to the U.S. without saying good-bye!" Or, every time I went to mail a letter home, the woman who worked at the Post Office and I would share with each other a little bit more about our lives. The lady who worked at the ice cream shop where I did my Spanish homework became one of my best friends. I became friends with all the bus drivers because I ran on the routes they drove. I was offered a friendly combination of wave, honk, and flashed lights as they drove by me. One week, I was running a bit early. The bus driver looked at his watch in confusion and gave me a big smile. Community matters. Relationships matter. It makes life more bearable, more enjoyable, and more beautiful. I was always struck by the power a bus honk had to brighten my day. We took the time to make each other visible. These were people who could have gone the whole year without acknowledging me; however, we humanized each other, and that made all the difference. I learned, then, that the best thing to do when I was feeling lonely is to realize that I am far from alone. Most people are genuinely compassionate, but sometimes I have to make the effort to show up and walk with the ladies.

Siete

These are the ones who say it's ridiculous to imagine that the world could be made better than it is... I fight that; I fight it as if I were drowning. When I come down to this feeling that I am an army of one standing on the broad plane waving my little flag of hope, I call up a friend or two and offer to make dinner for us. We remind ourselves that we aren't standing apart from the crowd, we are the crowd. We're a prairie fire, a church choir, a major note in the American chord...
We're the theater of the street, the accurate joy of children's hearts, the literature of tomorrow's wisdom arrived today, just in time. I'm with Emma Goldman: "Our revolution will have dancing— and excellent food. In the long run, the choice of life over death is too good to resist." [14]

BARBARA KINGSOLVER

For the duration of our conscious history, people have tried to control nature. Humans will go to great lengths—building dams, valves, and debris catchers to try to sway nature against its course. It has, at times, become an intense battle between ingenious human minds and the awesome power of the earth. Generally speaking, when humans let nature run its course, we see a cycle of destruction and rebirth, chaos and order, surplus and scarcity whose long-term effect, when summed up, is advantageous.

I witnessed this firsthand watching forest fires run their course in Colorado, witnessing the cycle of destruction and rebirth. Beyond that, nature's cycles remained intellectual for me. During my year in Uruguay, however, I learned to live through the cycles of my seasons there, deeply feeling abundance in its contrast to survival, laughter in its contrast to loneliness, and awakening in its contrast to hibernation. My life knew the extremes of joy and suffering more then than ever before. My life felt unbalanced. Over the course of the year, the ebbs and flows ran their course; and I became acutely aware that I could not, in any way, control them. This led ultimately to an advantageous sum.

Letting nature run its course in my life was petrifying–living through the dark times, while trusting that the light would come. For most of the year, Lascano symbolized scarcity, isolation, and introversion, while time with the other six volunteers meant guaranteed surplus, community, and extroversion. Tom was the closest, at five hours away. The others took twelve hours to get to, but they were the ones that kept me going. They were my cheerleaders, my confidants, my conversation partners, and my friends.

All this taught me so much about grace because they loved me when I needed it most, when I was at my worst. When I was paranoid, emotionally tapped out, frustrated, and dealing with mange and constipation, they continued to love me. To give you a glimpse into how seven strangers became best of friends over a year, let me tell you about wine country in Argentina.

One thing we did not want to be was a bunch of whiny martyrs. Yes, we all sacrificed a lot to get out of our comfort zones and live in South America for a year. Yes, we lived simply and exposed ourselves to brutal self-refinement. But we did it in style. In April, we all took a bus for over twenty hours into Mendoza, a region of central Argentina. We rented a house for a few days and traveled to learn a bit more about the vineyards. We sat on a blanket, making salami sandwiches at a lake lined with palm trees to celebrate Brooke's birthday. We cautiously descended a spiral staircase into the kitchen, surfacing for the first time at noon for the second day in a row. We listened to the Beastie Boys, Jack Johnson, Coldplay, and the Beatles on Tom's iPod hooked up to speakers. We watched *The Karate Kid* and counted how many times a mustachioed man appeared, while Alyson taught us about martial arts. We checked each other's heads for lice and took turns cooking amazing meals from the local market. Of course, we took a few very interesting wine tours. Malbec from Mendoza will always be my favorite wine, bottling up memories of thin spaces, little sips of perfection.

The women were in charge of giving me a sense of purpose, calling me their life coach as they told me about their years and I gently offered encouragement and objective insight. Brooke, Christine, Alyson, and I would swap sweaters when we got sick of the same two shirts. We would swap books and share thoughts. We sent each other encouraging notes and e-mails and came up with coping strategies for each other when times got hard.

The men were in charge of making me laugh, helping me unwind, and spinning experiences until I could get to the other side of them. They named me president of the men's club, and the four of us set out to conquer the South American nightlife. Tom, Andrew, Rob, and I deduced that part of really living there, becoming bicultural, required us to train until we could hang with South Americans socially. While we were all used to being fast asleep on a Saturday night by 2 a.m., that is just when South Americans are thinking about dinner. It took us all year because we did not see each other that much, but after several failed attempts when a bed would call our name all too soon, we finally spent a night on the town, South American style. I will present to you our winning strategy.

The night started out with our typical happy hour. At about four, we set out for a grocery store and came back to our home base with olives, chocolate, nuts, cheese, salami, crackers, beer, and wine. We checked in, laughed, and snacked for a few hours with Radiohead and Storyhill coming through our mini-speakers, a process we called "earning our nap." We napped until about 8:30 p.m., getting up gently to shower and converse while dancing to David Bowie and Freddie Mercury. We thought of the latest hour we could possibly conceive of to leave for dinner. Knowing this was still too early, we calculated an extra hour to that, leaving at 11:30 instead of 10:30 p.m., yet we did not go straight to dinner. After one beverage at a swanky bar with blue lighting, we finally headed to dinner around 1 a.m. when the city was just waking up. Leaving an amazing meal of pasta and wine, we made a necessary stop at 2:30 a.m. for dessert and coffee at an Indian-themed place with low couches and orange pillows so that we could use the second wind to our advantage. Arriving at our final destination at 4 a.m., we were worried that we had missed the rush; but it turns out we were unfashionably early. As we headed back, sweaty from dancing and completely exhausted at 8 a.m., it was almost as if we could hear the background music moving with us. We had finally done it. We had conquered South American nightlife.

We were all in charge of holding each other up, creating a sense of retreat where we could process and grow. They offered me a preview of what it would be like to return home to the United States, where comfort and commonality would surround me. These six will always be six of my best friends for walking with me through such a transformative time. Their companionship may have been the single biggest blessing of my year. They taught me the definition of community.

Returning to Lascano required twenty-six hours on several buses. I had plenty of time to start missing the good food and good laughter, adjusting to the survival after the abundance. I began the process of becoming my Spanish-speaking self, my Lascano self. I would shrink a bit and hunker in until the next time we all could get together. Times like these, little celebratory slices of heaven, kept me getting out of bed. They were weekends to look forward to. Somehow the other volunteers managed to rally around me and put me back together before sending me back to simple living and self-refinement.

Hospitality

After this the Lord appointed seventy others and sent them on ahead of him in pairs to every town and place where he himself intended to go. He said to them, "The harvest is plentiful, but the laborers are few; therefore ask the Lord of the harvest to send out laborers into the harvest. Go on your way. See, I am sending you out like lambs into the midst of wolves. Carry no purse, no bag, no sandals; and greet no one on the road. Whatever house you enter, first say, 'Peace to this house!' And if anyone is there who shares in peace, your peace will rest on that person; but if not, it will return to you. Remain in the same house, eating and drinking whatever they provide, for the laborer deserves to be paid. Do not move about from house to house. Whenever you enter a town and its people welcome you, eat what is set before you; cure the sick who are there, and say to them, 'The kingdom of God has come near to you.'"

LUKE 10:1–9

Vaccionces

The small plot of ground on which you were born cannot be
expected to stay forever the same. Each changes, and home becomes
different places. You took flesh from clay but the clay did not come
from just one place. To feel alive, important, and safe know your
own waters and hills, but know more. You have stars in your
bones and oceans in blood. You have opposing terrain in each eye.
You belong to the Land and sky of your first cry, you belong to
infinity.[1]

ALLA RENNE BOZARTH

During January, February, and March, Lascano offered me no
work. Because of the heat, the churches, schools, and, well, the entire
town shut down for summer. Everyone made enough money in nine
months to get by; and the hottest months found virtually no consumer
base, so the people of Lascano went to be close to the cooler ocean
breeze to survive the summer. My program coordinator wanted me
working, so I left Lascano on December 27th and finally returned on
March 7th. For the month of January, I was working at the church
camp in Palmares. Then I went on a ten-day vacation with my house
family to Northern Argentina, followed by ten days of vacation with
Dan. Next was a five-day church assembly in Western Uruguay and
a few days with Marina's family in that area. By mid-February, I was
spending time with each volunteer in Argentina, working at their sites.
My last stop on my way back to Lascano was at an orphanage.

In my months of being transient, I grew tired of transition and
transit, leaving me feeling numb. I also grew tired of lugging around
my backpack. It made me think more than ever about what I needed
and what I wanted. I wished I had have brought less so that I had
less to carry. Why does stuff make us feel less scared when facing a
time of the unknown? I learned the hard way that less is more, that
traveling lightly is beautiful, that you become what you carry.

One of my favorite parts of this time was getting to experience
the public transportation. For over a month, I stayed in each location
less than a week. I was always on the go, always fuzzy about where the
next bed would be, where the next meal would come from, and how

I would get myself from point A to point B by myself, in my second language. On the day I left my house family to meet the first volunteer in Buenos Aires, I took three buses, a boat, and a train, hauling my pack for miles in between. It was sometimes scary, sometimes fun, sometimes intimidating, but always an adventure. It helped when I knew that I had friends on the other side waiting for me.

With Andrew, I worked at La Casita, a home for boys. He was overworked as a volunteer, often one of the only consistent and loving presences in the lives of the seventeen boys who lived there. He was only there for a year. These boys were clever and tough, equipped with strong survival skills. They spent their days playing marbles and basketball. They ate off of Frisbees that were donated to be used as Frisbees, but were needed as plates. I was particularly struck by the story of four brothers whom I accompanied to the park and the river. Lucas, the oldest of the four, was eleven; Rodrigo, the youngest, was five. Matias and Esteban were in the middle. They were four of fourteen kids in a family, clearly from at least three different dads. Their mom simply dropped them off one day, probably never to return. They came underfed, with skin diseases and lice. Although they were well-fed and safe at La Casita, Lucas had an emotional breakdown the day I was there, still struggling with the realization that his mom was not returning and that, at eleven years of age, he was left to care for his three younger brothers. Rodrigo became a favorite of the North American volunteers. Cross-eyed and quiet, with an intense underbite, unending appetite, and the stocky build to prove it, he still carried with him the innocence of a five-year-old, not quite in touch with the gravity of his situation. These boys were just like other boys. They were beautiful and full of life. They liked being pushed on swings, tickled, and passed the soccer ball. It broke my heart to only spend a day with them, knowing I will always wonder how they are surviving in a world set up for them to fail.

With Alyson, I played bingo with lima beans in the company of six beautiful, elderly women. As I made rounds with Alyson at her nursing home placement, I was struck by the isolation, physical pain, and mental struggle of so many who lived there. After only giving a simple greeting, I was repeatedly met with overwhelming gratitude, affection, and compliments. Residents would clench my hand and kiss it while telling me how pretty I was and thanking me for stopping by to break the monotony of their day. In this one place, a plethora of wisdom came from years of experience. Elda, garnished in elegant jewelry, was a mother of five who spoke three languages. Atilio was a 1932 Olympic gold medalist in cycling from Italy. I met a man who had a stroke at the age of forty-two. He struggled with feeling useless and frustrated. Sadly, his wife did not come to see him often. With each encounter, I was freshly and acutely aware of how grateful each person was, simply to be seen and addressed. I hope they knew, too, how much their words and touch meant to me.

With Christine, I put lice caps on kids to prepare them to go swimming. We took about forty kids from the community center, where she worked, to a pool. I helped pass out lunch and made it a goal to leave without any severe injuries or concussions from diving and playing all day. I got a workout, walking through the pool with a minimum of three kids clinging, dangling, and giggling. Christine would offer quick, tragic back stories in English to help explain odd behavior and startling attachment issues. It was exhausting and good.

With Brooke, I baked bread with the women of her church. Every Thursday, the church provided ingredients, and the women made bread for their families for the week. While the bread was being kneaded, Brooke and I played checkers and drew dinosaurs with the young ones, held babies, and passed maté. In the afternoon, when the bread was finished, we all sat and shared a meal together, the long table packed with maternal energy and love. Dinner was basic—rice and more rice, with some bread on the side. While I struggled with eating all red meat and things like cow tongue and brain, Brooke struggled with only eating carbohydrates. But it filled us up all the same. From what I deduced, this was church at its best: meeting a need of the people while building community, then sharing in the breaking of bread together, a mixture of tangible and ritual sustenance.

My time of travel was exhausting, but full. I got to see different neighborhoods and different social service agencies that gave me a more complex view of Buenos Aires. It was rewarding to see the communities that my North American friends had carved out for themselves and to keep the people who had taught me about hospitality in my thoughts for the rest of the year.

Tias

The fruit of silence is prayer.
The fruit of prayer is faith.
The fruit of faith is love.

The fruit of love is service.
The fruit of service is peace.[2]

MOTHER TERESA

Many of my friends and family, when hearing I was off to Uruguay to work with children for a year, were convinced I would come back with a newly adopted son or daughter of my own. In March, I was in a situation to be tempted to do just that. My first week of March was spent at Hogar Nimmo in Colonia Sacramento, Uruguay. It is a social service agency of the Waldensien Church trying to create a sense of community, family, and home for kids with no safe space to call their own. Thirty children lived there, creating two neighboring families of fifteen. All of the kids struggled with life, carrying some of the most heart-wrenching stories I have ever heard. All of the kids fit into either the category of cute, precious, beautiful, stunning, or gorgeous. They climbed on my lap instantly. I was loved quickly and well.

On staff were two administrators, a tutor, a psychologist, a cook, a cleaner, a man who tended to the land and taught the kids how to raise the animals, and four women who were intentionally and affectionately referred to as aunts. Two aunts stayed for four days and nights followed by two who came for the remaining three days to try and offer the children some stability and sense of parenting. Can you imagine being a mom to fifteen kids with special needs? These women were amazing.

Over the course of the week, amidst drinking maté with the aunts, translating English songs into Spanish for the teenagers, playing soccer with the boys, and pushing the little ones on the swings, slowly I started to hear the stories of how these thirty children came to live at the Hogar. To my surprise, a good number of the children were not orphans. Parents stopped by and even took their sons or daughters for the day. Marco lived at the Hogar with three of his seven siblings. His mom, who lived four hours away, called every Sunday to talk to them. She had decided that seven kids were too many, so picked four to drop off one day and never looked back. When I asked the aunts why all of the children lived in the Hogar and not with mom or dad, they answered, "We just don't know. We show up and love these kids as best as we can and try not to ask too many questions. We will never understand."

Other children were orphans. Matias was a three-year-old who would sprint across the grounds with windmill arms to give me a hug each morning. He loved to climb on my lap, pet my hair, and get pushed on the swings. At least ten times a day, he would look up at me with unassuming eyes and ask in his precious lisp, "What ith my mom'th name?" I had to tell him repeatedly that I just did not know. He may always be left to wonder. Enso was a five-year-old with a wild imagination. He told me story after story about his house, his parents, his grandparents, and his farm. The aunts told me that he was locked in his house for four days and, although bruised and malnourished, finally escaped through a window and got help at the neighbor's house. His made-up stories of family and home, which he will never see again, were survival mechanisms for him. His sister, Diana, was one year and three months. She arrived as an eight-month-old unable to crawl, but with the help of food and exercises she was waddling around like a future marathoner. Along with the two-year-old twins, Floppy and Carolina, these five will probably never see their parents again. However, the aunts and older children at the Hogar are living in a way that will offer these children love and stability that they will all grow up to cherish and appreciate.

Every minute I spent with these children was meaningful. They loved easily and passionately, soaking up attention, affection, and compliments. I will often think back to the moments helping the aunts cut nails, cut hair, and organize school supplies to prepare the twenty-five oldest for the first day of school. As they all came out standing tall in their best clothes with their freshly showered hair and new backpacks, I actually cried as I sent them off to school, anxiously awaiting their stories and hugs upon their return. I will remember sitting with the eighteen-month-old twins as it got late, one on each knee, them clutching my fingers and leaning against my chest for support. I will remember going on walks and playing soccer, being shown pet animals, being welcomed to dinner, and being embraced after a good first day at school. I will remember eight- year-olds cleaning the floor, nine-year-olds tending to the baby cats, and three-year-olds protecting two-year-olds like a dysfunctional, beautiful family doing their best to get love and get by. They were precious survivors, and it was difficult to leave after being taught so much by them for only a week. I know that if I ever get pessimistic or apathetic in the face of the human condition, I will call to mind those aunts who invest so much time and love to make sure those kids have a happy and safe future.

September 23
I have been challenged this year to let God be who God wants to be. I hold on tightly to my aloneness, cling to the ugly, embarrassing parts of myself, hoping God will not see. Where I need to be touched the most by

God, the places where the most pain lies, those are the places I fortify so that God will not seep in. I hide from God the places where I experience feelings of guilt, shame, confusion, and loss. Instead of God being with me in my vulnerability, I choose to stay alone. I know that God wants to be my companion this year, because God became Jesus, who came to live among us. But my actions do not always reflect that knowledge.

Idiomas

The world into which you were born...is just one model of reality... [O]ther societies of the world are not failed attempts at modernity. They are unique manifestations of the human spirit.[3]

WADE DAVIS

I spent one week of February at the Annual Synod Assembly Meeting of the Waldensian Church. The meeting was a real turning point for me for a few reasons. One, I got to see the Church I was working for as a whole. This Church broke away from the Roman Catholic Church three hundred years before Luther, believing that the Bible should be translated and shared with all people regardless of gender, race, or class. In Argentina and Uruguay there remains a scattered 3,000 loyal and passionate Waldensian people whose ancestors fled persecution in the Piedmont Valley. I observed the Church to be like a family in its intimacy and honesty. They had a history of being persecuted, and they clung to their heritage for strength. They liked being small, spread out, and family-oriented. The Church seems to have a beautiful way of distributing power gracefully so that no one person has all of it. New people are always up front. The meeting was quirky and refreshingly low key. At one point, the lights went out, and they used candles. They voted for things by raising a little piece of purple paper in favor. I tried to imagine the Roman Catholic Church having a meeting where no person was clearly in charge, worship included women preaching, and voting was done with purple construction paper. Not in my lifetime.

Second, many people I met there took me very seriously, unlike people in Lascano. I felt like an equal with something to offer. One man encouraged me by telling me about the violence in the lives of the kids in Lascano. He told me that my presence was offering them a new model, which plants seeds and makes a difference. People from all over Argentina and Uruguay invited me to come to their churches and social service agencies to learn more about what they do. I felt like I had mentors and peers who were opening me up instead of closing me down.

Third, this was my first real experience of having South American peers. Lascano had very few people my age. Some were studying in Montevideo. For those who stopped studying, twenty-five-year-olds were either in the fields working or busy with multiple children. I found my friends, then, to be a mixture of teenagers and young moms I met at the preschool. The church meeting was the first time I remember from the year abroad really making foreign friends my age. They reminded me what it felt like to have easy, interesting social interaction. They found me each morning to say hello and grabbed me each night to join them for a beer or for guitar playing by the water. They saw me, enjoyed me, and appreciated what I had to offer, while giving me relaxation and laughter.

Finally, for the first time that year, I felt bilingual. My favorite moment happened over lunch on the last day. I was invited to sit across from a man from central Uruguay named Dario. He wanted to practice his English because he was going to the United States to give a speech on the idea of empire and needed to brush up. Next to him sat a man from Argentina who was going to the same conference, but he told me, "You speak Spanish because you are in Uruguay. I will speak English when I get to the United States." Fair enough. To my left was a man named Stefano from Italy who I had become friends with throughout the week despite both of us using our second language. To my right was a man from France who could barely speak Spanish, but did speak English fairly well. So over lunch, people from five countries communicated in three languages. The Italian spoke French to the Frenchman; the Frenchman, Uruguayan, and I spoke English; and I spoke Spanish to the Argentine and Italian. And the tower of Babel came tumbling down. As I flowed easily from English to Spanish over topics of theology and politics, I truly felt for the first time that I was bilingual and that the skill was needed and helpful in the conversation. The French man needed my English, while the Uruguayan wanted to hear it. The world began to feel a bit more interconnected as language barriers were broken and people previously separated were able to speak.

Our last night of the meeting featured worship with singing and dancing. Person after person approached me with hugs and well wishes. I reflected on the fullness of the last week, and I was grateful.

Pan

*One of the greatest evils of the day…is [the] sense of futility.
Young people say, "What good can one person do? What is the
sense of our small effort?" They cannot see that we must lay one
brick at a time, take one step at a time, we can be responsible only
for the one action of the present moment. But we can beg for an
increase of love in our hearts that will vitalize and transform all
our individual actions, and know that God will take them and
multiply them, just as Jesus multiplied the loaves and fishes.*[4]

DOROTHY DAY

When praying to God for daily bread, I never even knew what
that meant. Plenty of times in my life I had stopped eating, in fact,
and carried on just fine. But I am forever grateful for a year that taught
me what daily bread truly is.

The bread in Lascano was amazing. We ate it for breakfast, snacks,
and dinner. It became a sustaining staple for me that I looked forward
to a great deal. The harsh red meat was brutal to my stomach, but the
bread calmed me. Marcelo would swing by the bakery almost every
day to get bread for the kids who came to church after school and
for his family. Across Uruguay, this same bread was a part of every
meal. It resembled a slightly stretched slinky, a six inch tall cylinder
with multiple grooves showing where the bread could be torn to
make discs perfect for spreading butter, jam, or *dulce de leche* on. It was
flaky on the outside and soft on the inside, best when fresh. It was not
necessarily hearty, dense, or nutrition packed. It did not carry with it
the ability to fill one up, but it did the trick as a side. The cook would
normally disperse two or three across the table for the group to tear
at and use as a fork or to soak up straggling rice or sauce.

Not having much money and living with a family, I ate what I was
given when it was given to me. Often, not knowing exactly what was
coming next, my sense of daily bread changed. I was acutely thankful
for being fed. More than just food was involved. I was thankful for
whatever sustained me throughout my day, whether it was bread, or
a letter from a friend back home, or a good conversation in Spanish,
or prayer. My daily bread would be something different every day,
but for the whole year, it constantly came. I was sustained.

Every day we fed bread and milk to the kids in the after-school
program. Most came very hungry and ate a lot. Sometimes, that bread

was the last thing they ate until the next day. It was very powerful for me to share bread with them. Even on the hard days, I can hope that maybe I made someone's day a little easier with an offering of tasty bread. If that empowered them to stand a little taller and live a little bigger, then that communion we shared for snack was a way for me to live the gospel.

Orlando

It is enough to meet Orlando.

TOM

Meeting Orlando was sufficient payback for Tom's year in South America. Had that been the year's only positive experience, Tom would have been glad he had gone. Orlando is a mechanic in Lascano who is very active in the Waldensian Church. He is a simple man who works hard and loves his family. Orlando welcomed Tom into his house each time he traveled from Montevideo to Lascano to see me. He loved his town, loved his life, and took the time to make us always feel welcome. So often in Lascano, especially at the beginning, I would sit through meetings or church and feel a bit invisible. No one would talk to me; and, not knowing where I fit in, I had a hard time finding my voice. Every time Orlando was present, I knew I would not feel invisible. He would turn to me and ask me to offer my opinion to the group, or he would offer up a prayer of thanksgiving for my presence during worship. I never felt invisible when he was around. He understood, somehow, that it was important to both of us that I was there, and we tried to teach and learn from each other every day.

Orlando made an effort to connect with me every chance he got. He genuinely wanted to hear my opinion on fascinating questions such as, "What is it like watching news about your country from here?" or, "What do you see about our culture that you think we could improve on?" He constantly reminded me that he thought it was a beautiful gesture for me to leave my family to come and live in Uruguay. He loved the sharing of cultures, the mutual learning, the conversations about language, and the comparing and sharing of lives. I knew very early on that he would be a highlight of the year for me–his mustache and dirty mechanic fingernails and genuine, untiring interest in my year, my work, and me. Orlando works hard,

loves his family, and supports his church. He represents, for me, all
that is good, honorable, and right in the world. He speaks and seeks
truth always. It is exhausting to make sure the people on the outside
of things feel seen and heard, but he gracefully and quietly made
that his quest.

On Tom's second trip to Lascano, Orlando took us out for the
day to teach us about the process of harvesting rice, a huge part of
Lascano's economy. We saw the fields and the factories, stopped at
the ocean (where the sand was so dense we drove on it), crossed a
river on a ferry that we drove our car onto, stopped by the office
where Orlando does his work on field equipment, and watched his
niece play in a big band for the town celebration.

On our way home, Tom and I were sitting in the back of Orlando's
car with Orlando's four-year-old grandchild, Facundo, sleeping
between us. Six of us occupied a car that seated four. The car had
no internal paneling, working radio, or seatbelts—but it ran. Flowers
and berries that Orlando had picked for me from the side of the road
sat to my right. My job was passing maté, which proved to be quite
difficult on the gravel road. The sun was setting, turning the sky into
God's orchestra of pinks, oranges, and purples. Palm trees bowed
to us in reverence as cows milled about. The silence in the car was
saturated with the joyful contentment of family and love. Tom and I
looked at each other and smiled, each knowing the other was actively
soaking up every moment to pull out years down the road, when our
memories of Uruguay would begin to fade. Orlando had actively
pulled Tom and me into his world, and we came to appreciate with
him as our enthusiastic teacher.

June 3

*I have learned a lot about traveling with integrity. It is usually
stressful, often taxing, offering much down time, calling me to use much
common sense, to be flexible, to check my attitude, to trust that everything
will work out. Traveling is a constant invitation to close down or open
up. I have learned to bear annoyances with dignity, to be content in the
moment, to keep my mind on things such as God, loved ones, and fond
memories so that I can remain in a space of my highest values, making
it easier to remember my true identity. I challenge myself to see beauty
in every face on the journey, which helps me respond to people with
compassion and patience. The more I let my light shine and invite the
light of others to shine, the more the light shows up on the path, lighting
the way for a smoother ride. It can be a smile, or a hello, letting people
go ahead of me if they are in a hurry, walking mindfully through stations*

and terminals, enjoying the process. This year, this life, I am traveling
without arriving. Knowing that keeps me from getting anxious, from taking
out little frustrations on people who did not set out to upset me. Traveling,
like life, is a constant invitation to connect and see beauty, to give and
receive light on the path.

Profesora

A woman who teaches by being.

MAYA ANGELOU

Early in the year, when I sensed that language was going to be a
major barrier, I asked Marcelo and Marina for help finding a Spanish
teacher. Seven months in, when I had almost given up hope of it ever
happening, Dinorah offered to bring me over to the house of a friend
whose mom taught English. In March, I started classes with Maria
José. I was so excited to hone my speaking skills to communicate
at a deeper level. The day I went to meet her, I had no idea what a
blessing her presence in my life would be.

On our first meeting, she invited me into her home, handed
me some tea, and asked me to tell her my story. She taught students
English and was excited to try to teach me Spanish. She told me that
she was from Montevideo originally and moved to Lascano fifteen
years prior. She explained that she still got treated like an outsider,
describing the town as very closed-minded and excluding in nature.
It was a good validation of what I had been feeling.

The longer I went to class at the house of Maria José, the closer
we became. She became my confidant, asking me questions initially to
get me speaking more, but then progressively becoming my mentor,
my counselor, and friend. Her living room table became safe for me.
As I shared more about myself, she, too, shared from her experiences.
Class became a sanctuary, a place of respite, home.

One day I was so frustrated about what was happening outside
her living room that I could not handle the subjunctive verb tense
inside of her living room. Totally embarrassed, I started to cry and
could not stop. She tried to comfort me about my Spanish, telling
me that the subjunctive is not worth tears. That made me laugh, and
I began to tell her where my heart was, too preoccupied to worry

about Spanish. The floodgates opened. I think she realized then that what happened at her house was not about learning verb tenses. It was not about learning a language. It was an objective place where I could share my feelings and frustrations. Because Marcelo was my house father, boss, and pastor, I did not know to whom I might go with personal concerns. This situation made me feel more and more isolated. She understood. That was the one time she let me break my Spanish and speak in English. After that, she started each class asking me how I was doing and putting extra effort toward advocating for me and empowering me to advocate for myself.

Her home was always warm and calm. She always invited me to sit, drink tea, and chat. I was always received with respect, love, and gentleness. I tentatively opened up to her and let her open up to me, all the while getting better at Spanish. I always left class full of the Spirit and feeling loved, cared for, and nurtured. She was an unexpected gift. It took seven months, but I finally found an objective advocate that I could talk to about my concerns and feelings in confidence.

Space is important, and I never really had one space I could call my own. I experienced what so many in the world do: the struggle of being transient, of not having a physical space to call home, a space where guards are let down and comfort and safety abound. We all need spaces where we can find rest, spaces where we feel safe to cry. It took me seventh months to find, but the living room table in the house of Maria José was that space for me in Uruguay.

> We are all longing to go home to some place we have never been—a place, half-remembered, and half-envisioned we can only catch glimpses of from time to time. Community. Somewhere, there are people to whom we can speak with passion without having words catch in our throats. Somewhere a circle of hands will open to receive us, eyes will light up as we enter, voices will celebrate with us whenever we come into our own power. Community means strength that joins our strength to do the work that needs to be done. Arms to hold us when we falter. A circle of healing. A circle of friends. Someplace where we can be free.[5]
>
> STARHAWK

Ellie's second house family (l-r): Mario, Iris, Julia, Ellie, and Mariana at her twenty-sixth birthday celebration (p.138).

The view heading into town from the route of Lascano, Rocha, Uruguay (p.17).

Machie, an orphan at Hogar Nimo, adjusts his uniform for the first day of school (p.86).

Grade school children of Lascano dance at the end-of-the-year celebration (p.135)

Breathtaking waterfalls
at the National Park in Iguazú, Argentina (p.141).

Four-year-old preschoolers take a break from recess to snap a photo (p.134).

Three maté gourds, a thermos, and a carrying case Ellie was given during the year (p.59).

A quaint vineyard in the mountains of northern Argentina (p.78).

Lascano kids gather at Ellie's farewell fiesta (p.58).

Intricate woven fabrics displayed at a typical Argentine market (p.102).

A common home in Lascano that could easily catch fire in the winter (p.19).

Juliana Allio, Ellie's Uruguayan niece (p.147).

Brokenness

*My Lord God, I have no idea where I am going. I do not see the
road ahead of me. I cannot know for certain where it will end.
Nor do I really know myself, and the fact that I think that I am
following your will does not mean that I am actually doing so.
But I believe that the desire to please you does in fact please you.
And I hope I have that desire in all that I am doing. I hope that I
will never do anything apart from that desire. And I know that if
I do this you will lead me by the right road, though I may know
nothing about it. Therefore will I trust you always though I seem
to be lost and in the shadow of death. I will not fear, for you
are ever with me, and you will never leave me to face my perils
alone.*[1]

THOMAS MERTON

April 12

*If someone were to come here, I do not think he or she would get it
right away. The darkness of Lascano seeps and crawls and saturates. It
gets under my skin and into my bones and clings until I can't breathe. And
I never knew I let it in. It stops my digestive system and clogs my sinuses.
It makes my eyelids heavy, sits at the bottom of my heart, and pushes on
my lungs. It lifts the second I leave town. I look up and can breathe fully.
I uncurl my shoulders and find my voice. It is the dirt, the depression,
the status quo, the apathy, the unfriendly town that has no interest in
breaking out; the stagnant, suffocating violence that happens behind
closed doors. The inevitability here lurks behind the failure to transform.
Last night I reached out, but there was no one there. There is not a single
person I can go to here for comfort or touch, for tears or laughter. There
is no healing, no safe space, no community. I have learned enough, been
through enough. I have been praying for hope, light and transformation
for eight months. Nothing is going to change. All the high, theological
thoughts I came in with are laughable now. Hitting the brick wall is*

causing me brain damage, I hope not permanently. Some bridges need to be burned. Some relationships need to die. Sometimes walking away is the best thing. Lascano is through with me and I am through with it. I have paid my dues. I have failed. Please have mercy on me.

Silencio

When it is genuine, when it is born of the need to speak, no one can stop the human voice. When denied a mouth, it speaks with the hands or the eyes, or the pores, or anything at all. Because every single one of us has something to say to the others, something that deserves to be celebrated or forgiven by others.[2]

EDUARDO GALEANO

So often things will make sense in hindsight. Healing comes with being able to put all the pieces together in a continuous, logical story. But in the moment, the unexplainable can be maddening. In hindsight, I would love to take back one moment in my year, to act differently with the knowledge I did not have then but do have now. That one moment happened in Palmares.

My house family and I had two days alone together in Palmares in between camp one and two. On the first day after breakfast, we headed down to the beach. I made sure Ignacio and Santiago had pails and shovels, hats and towels, and, of course, a soccer ball. In my bikini and shorts on our walk to the ocean, I chatted with Marcelo about the first camp. We had set up camp, and the kids ran into the water. I sat down to watch. Marina joined us a few minutes later, clearly in an unpleasant mood. Not knowing that I was the cause of her mood, I stood up and sat down closer to her and Dinorah on the beach. She spun away from me, talking to her daughter in low tones that I could not pick up with her back to me. Shortly after, she got up and headed back. Marcelo ran after her and put his arm around her. She threw it off barking at him again in words I could not understand at a distance.

I remained a bit confused until the next morning. When Ignacio was anxious to get down to the water that next day, Marcelo made clear eye contact with me as he told his son, "Not yet. We have to wait for your mother. She does not like for us to go without her." Enough said. I felt inconsiderate, but the punishment she handed me seemed cruel and exaggerated. That is when the silence started.

The next moment that I would have changed happened on the first day of family vacation, as we set up our tent at a campsite that had a pool. Exhausted from heat, I jumped in the pool, but sensed this same coldness from Marina as she sat and watched me teach her son how to swim. I felt like I could not win. I had to keep living my life even if that made her uncomfortable, right?

If I knew then what I know now, I would have put a T-shirt on over my suit, waited for Marina, and talked to her children instead of her husband on the walk down to the beach. I would have sat with Marina, who is afraid to swim, and made conversation instead of jumping in with Marcelo and Santi. For months after, I did not have the luxury of even hindsight, since Marina stopped talking to me; and the unexplainable was indeed maddening.

Including Marcelo's mom and dad, who lived in Entre Rios, Argentina, eight of us were on vacation when I gave Santi swimming lessons. The daily schedule became two cars, four people in each, driving for most of the day in Northern Argentina, then stopping at six to eat dinner and set up tents to sleep in. We had a lot of ground to cover. This meant a lot of silence. Early on, Marina made it very clear to me that it would be better if I rode with the grandparents, so I found myself in the backseat of a stranger's car driving for about eight hours a day. I would sit in silence wondering what the lives of the people we passed by were like. *How did they get there? Will they ever leave? What are their normal days like? I realize that I could live just about anywhere. Maybe they cannot, but why here? Why did that man choose a pink cement house with these chickens and that clothes wire in Rio de Hongo, Argentina?*

As vacation wore on, I became hungry for interaction. I would literally go days with no one talking to me unless to answer a question with a short, curt response. My "Good morning" would not be answered. I asked how people were, but was never asked how I was. It bothered me, but I was in the mountains of Argentina. Creation was filling me up. I had my survival kit of book, music, and journal. The contrast between the beauty of the world and weight of the silence, however, was striking. I tried not to be the victim. I just kept making excuses for Marina's silence, telling myself that family vacation can be stressful, and I was sure that it was worse because I was there. Yet this voice inside me knew how I would welcome someone into my family. I did not think I was asking for too much just to be addressed now and again.

Two small patterns put an exclamation point on the silence. First, Marina stopped passing me maté. Culturally, it was just an ugly thing to do. Maté is used to break barriers, to connect with strangers, yet their own housedaughter was getting excluded. I finally worked up the courage to ask Marina if I could have some. She said yes, then never passed it. Second, I was not asked to be in a single picture during a ten-day vacation when dozens were snapped. I started offering to take pictures for them to make myself feel better. It was good to feel useful and sad to feel so markedly outside the family, like I did not belong and they wanted to make sure I knew it. They wanted family pictures, and that did not in any way include me, not even for that year. They wished I were not there, that I had never come to stay with them. Their silence confirmed it. Ignacio would look at pictures years from now and forget that I was there. Maybe a tourist from Chile had offered to snap a shot for them. Most of my pictures from vacation were of the old, calm, wise, strong, and fertile mountains or the sheep and goats, small towns and foothills with no people at all. From my vantage point, I was alone.

Was one moment on a beach and one in a pool really the cause of such a long-standing silent treatment? Was it my fault? I will never know. No words were spoken to me, and I did not bridge the silence because of my insecurity with Spanish. I felt like the biggest burden this family had ever known. But we were stuck in a car together, so I chose to take in the mountains and try with all my might to turn my intuition off.

I got violently ill at the end of vacation. Marina blamed it on me drinking a beer at dinner. Although she made me feel like a little kid, I just accepted her theory and told her I would only drink water for a few days. I realized it required me to be losing scary amounts of fluid for her to pay attention to me. So you can imagine the relief to leave them after ten days of vacation for time with the other volunteers in Argentina. I would only see them for one other week in my summer time away from Lascano. As I sat at the train station with my book and a coffee, the peace was overwhelming. I felt so much less alone when I was by myself compared to the suffocating silence of my host mother.

Marcelo had to be at the week-long church meeting that I went to, so he brought the extended family, but I rarely interacted with them. It was poignant for me that I was being taken care of so well by strangers at the meeting while the people I knew the best ignored me. I approached Marcelo every day to say hello, but that was the extent of our interactions. During a break, I found my host family on the riverbed and tried to make conversation, but they told me they were fine and sat in awkward silence until I left. At that moment I started taking my interpretation of the situation seriously. I was not the problem. I had not changed. I was interacting with the people in the meeting how I normally interact with human beings. I showed interest and respect and got treated with dignity in return. It was not a cultural difference or a language barrier. I was not making it up. They might be shy or awkward, but that was no excuse for making me feel silenced and invisible, yet also an annoying burden. I had a glimpse of abundance at the meeting, but was quickly back to surviving the silence of the family.

I returned home to Lascano in March, with five months to go. Initially, it felt great to be in one place. As I unpacked, memories from my first night back in September came flashing back. I was proud at how far I had come. It was odd being back, running with the cows, getting stares, seeing horses on the street, getting waves from truck drivers, seeing birds again. But it did not take long for all the struggles to come back, too. By the first dinner, I was reawakened to the silence, feeling like an annoying observer. I was surprised that nothing had changed, shocked that we would coexist like this for five more months.

My Spanish had improved a great deal since a few months prior when I left the house for summer. I now began to accept that the silence was not a cultural barrier, and it was not in my head. It was real. Marina could no longer talk under her breath and know I would not follow, so she stopped talking when I was around almost completely. Marcelo told me they were going to Ombues for Holy Week (interesting time for the pastor to take vacation), and I came home from work one day to an empty house. I never had my own space. I rushed home from work each day like an excited little kid. I kept the Cartoon Network off and put on music and sang out loud. I listened to my own voice, which I had not heard in awhile. I realized, yet again, how deprived I had been. My host family did not invite me to be me. They had a special way of making me feel constantly apologetic as a nuisance. I made my own food and ate it slowly, quietly, and soaked in the lack of yelling, hurrying, and animal fat. I chose the portion and the pace.

While they were gone, I looked forward to my day. I was excited to get out of bed and play my music, breathe and move and have my being without being apologetic. No one made me feel like a stranger. I felt twenty-five again. The fear—which I did not even know was fear—had fallen away. The day before they returned, I spent the entire morning drawing. I had always been a left-brain dominant person, but what I was experiencing was not getting out in words. I wanted color over paragraph structure. I wanted blurred lines not perfection, process not product. I needed to express without being concise. Without thinking, I put my gut out on paper for hours. I created and played, blurred lines and processed. Some drawings were physically taxing, none had premeditated visions before they appeared. When I put the charcoal down, exhausted, I looked and was struck by what I had released. I could see my feelings on paper, which somehow validated them for me. A lot of color was trapped by black lines.

I was lying in bed trying to sleep at midnight when they came home. The feeling that started crawling all over my insides—a combination of dread, inevitability, annoyance, and depression—was consuming. I felt myself go back into hibernation, survival mode. I could feel my world shrinking again. I started counting immediately the days until I left to go see the other volunteers, until I returned home. The time that seemed like nothing earlier that day instantly felt like forever. What was joyful silence for a few days became heavy and constricting silence. I said good morning and got no response. I ate cow jaw for lunch. I went back to tiptoeing, not sure where to step, back to status quo.

After getting no help from my country supervisor, I started talking to Marcelo about changing houses. He said there were no prospects, although I sensed he did not try hard to find them. I started putting feelers out, but at times I would second-guess my decision to break free. I would come up with a good question that could not be answered with yes or no, and Marcelo and Marina would have an hour-long conversation with me about the dictatorship or the church. Then I would start feeling guilty and rethink all that I could do better to help the relationship. I could put forth more effort and be more present. I tried to communicate more directly and do more chores around the house to earn my keep. I tried to fix something that I did not even understand the brokenness of.

When guests from the greater Church came to do workshops and spend the night, I saw them receive the outgoing, pleasantly superficial version of the couple. I was not an outsider anymore, so I no longer got the treatment. Yet I was not family, so I could not be yelled at. I was stuck in the middle, tolerated at best, noticeably ignored and avoided. I came home and did not receive a hello or, "How was your day?" Eyes downcast, I would finish talking to my family on the phone, and laughter would stop, the T.V. suddenly mesmerizing. They never let me talk about my grandpa dying, Dan coming to visit, or why, with only five months until my job ended, they still had no vision of my role in the church.

By the beginning of May, I had hit rock bottom. I was having contrasting experiences outside that validated my hurt inside the home. I was having very positive interactions with people I was building relationships with, and I was finding work for myself, so I grew confident in the fact that I was not, indeed, the problem. I was interacting with people outside the home how I normally did, with human decency. Even though this family had welcomed me in the beginning, even though Marcelo was my pastor, boss, and father, I simply could not be ignored for three more months. They informed me that we were going to Ombues on a Wednesday, and I decided that was my chance to either turn things around or walk away knowing I had done all that I could to make it work.

Small moments in Ombues were beautiful. Ignacio crawled onto my lap to watch a movie. I played checkers with Santiago for hours. I took a turn around town with Dinorah and talked to her about her love life. The uncles joked with me and asked if I was ready to go back to the United States. One morning, Marcelo even asked me how I was feeling. But on the whole, it was more of the same. One day, as an experiment, I said nothing for twenty-four hours. The only thing said to me that day came from an aunt, who offered, "Ellie, you have gotten fat. Have you stopped running?" I was emotionally prepared, then, to accept the gift of grace through an invitation.

Shortly after we returned, Mario and Julia, the parents of my friend and yoga student Mariana, invited me to come live in their home for the rest of my stay. I said yes. Walking across town with my travel backpack on, I felt physical liberation in a way I had never known. I never turned back, and their door was never opened to me again. I walked away from the only thing I had known for my first eight months with the hope of something better, still not understanding what, if anything I had done wrong.

What I thought was ungrounded punishment for one moment at the beach and one moment in a pool made complete sense a month later when I was informed that Marina struggles with serious, yet legitimate, jealousy issues due to dealings Marcelo had with women in his previous church. Marina stopped talking to me out of jealousy. In turn her husband—my boss and pastor—stopped talking to me to save his marriage. It seemed irrational and cruel in the moment, but, when given their marriage history, I instantly found understanding and compassion for Marina. That is why her extended family, especially the sisters, shut me out too. That is why members of Marcelo's old church looked deep into my eyes with knowing concern when they asked me how my year in Lascano was going. Everybody but me knew the story.

Being a young, single woman from the United States, I should have never been placed in their home, in their church, or maybe even their town. The silence was laced with sin, lack of healing and communication, old baggage, none of which I could glean with my lack of language skills. Not knowing the dynamics I was walking into, I was not as overly sensitive or intentional as I would have been if someone had told me the fragile dynamic. I was stuck in a household with old hurt, and walking away was the best thing that I could do for them and me. I immediately flourished outside the weight of the silence. Unfortunately, because of these dynamics, my year was not as much about church work or justice issues, but about emotional survival, self-advocacy, and coping strategy.

May 2
Sometimes I don't pray. Because I can't, because it is not built into the community here, because I do not know what to say. But it is always better when I do pray. Always. And it is nice to know that when I cannot find the words, people at home can while I am looking.

Hola

Only fear can defeat life.[3]

YANN MARTEL

In the fall, my town grew from 2,500 people to 9,000. It was harvest time for rice, so migrant workers arrived in Lascano and the surrounding region in March. Every year the local government deals with the issues surrounding illegal Brazilians crossing the border to work for cheaper wages, and overworked and underpaid Uruguayans living in their trucks and occasionally causing problems.

When I first arrived in Lascano, I did not feel very welcomed as an outsider. Not only was I not from Lascano, I was from the United States. I got stared at a lot, which was unnerving and scary. Boys stopped playing and just watched. Men slowed their cars down and stuck their heads out the window and turned as they passed. A woman passed me where there was not a single other soul in sight and would not say hi. Sometimes I did not notice. Sometimes I said hello, while other times I stared back—with a smile on a good day. Sometimes I just put my head down and kept walking. Somehow, the silent stares made me feel dirty, weird, and white. I wanted to shut the blonde off and hide, or blend in or cry or stay inside. It was so tiring being the other.

Seven months into my stay there, things had improved immensely due to my continuous effort to build relationships, to undo stereotypes people may have attached to my nationality. For example, many women used to walk by me and stare, or maybe answer my, "Hola," with an unenthusiastic and obligatory, "Hola," in response. Eventually, those same women would stop and talk to me, recognizing that I was that North American girl who adored their sons and daughters who I had as students. Kids saw my white skin and blonde hair. They asked questions and wanted to touch it to see if it was real, but they did not have any judgment attached to it yet. Children love easily, and I was able to use my relationship with the kids to build relationship with the adults.

With a new crew in town, however, I felt the stares again. It was very scary and objectifying, having male strangers unnerve me with their unwavering looks. Some looks were sexual, some carried disgust, others amusement, and many just confusion. I felt very much like the other, very disconnected and two-dimensional. I wondered what thoughts were running through their heads and what labels and assumptions were being projected on me. I changed my running routes to avoid their trucks and hangouts. I focused on our differences instead of our similarities, and the boundaries and barriers that kept us coexisting, but not conversing. They were male, transient, poor, strong, Spanish-speaking, and working like crazy. I was not. I stayed in more and started pulling inside of myself again. I remembered why I was scared to leave the house during my first months. I hated the staring and never got over it. I felt dirty, tired, and sad more often again, thinking all the progress I had made to feel comfortable and accepted and humanized had been erased. On bad days, I just put my head down and felt their eyes burning in my back. The barriers remained, and the silence was deafening.

Then I remembered what helped me build relationship in the first place. I imagined that I would be welcomed and approached in Lascano, but I had to take initiative and find the courage to approach the stranger. I got to work, starting to break the stare with a simple, "Hola." I worked up to courage to say hello, knowing in time as we became human to each other, the potential hatred, objectification, and misunderstanding that could come from difference, judgment, and silence might well be replaced by conversation; humanization; and–hopefully–mutual respect, friendship, and learning. And that is what happened. Instead of stares, I began to encounter small interactions. With a simple hello, I stepped through the barriers to find people who were more like me than not. The fear lessened, and I settled back in to the place I was starting to call home.

October 24

There is something about how clearly European Montevideo and Buenos Aires are that makes me sad. They are cities so clearly the result of the conquerors coming from Spain to South America. I guess it is the same in our country, and it makes me think what it would look like if the conquerors listened instead of spoke, learned instead of taught. That is what I struggle with here, too. I do not want Lascano to change because I lived there for a year. I want to change because I lived in Lascano. It does have something to teach me. I want to become more bilingual and bicultural so that I can flourish in both places. I have a great opportunity to change and adapt here. It is painful, and it will be painful upon my return. It is difficult to fight the urge to assert myself daily, daily grieving my ineffectiveness and my ability solely to take up space. Daily feeling so North American and so alone. I do not know what I will learn from this place. I do not know what I will teach them. But, most importantly, I pray that it will be done in love, which takes time and courage. This place will become part of me, and I will have to honor that part of me when I return.

Marcadora

The paradox of our time in history is that we have taller buildings, but shorter tempers; wider freeways, but narrower viewpoints. We spend more, but have less; we buy more, but enjoy it less. We have bigger houses and smaller families; more conveniences, but less time; we have more degrees, but less sense; more knowledge but less judgment; more experts, but more problems; more medicine, but less wellness. We drink too much, smoke too much, spend too recklessly, laugh too little, drive too fast, get too angry too quickly, stay up too late, get up too tired, read too seldom, watch TV too much, and pray too seldom. We have multiplied our possessions, but reduced our values. We talk too much, love too seldom, and hate too often. We've learned how to make a living, but not a life; we've added years to life, not life to years. We've been all the way to the moon and back, but have trouble crossing the street to meet the new neighbor. We've conquered outer space, but not our inner space. We've done larger things, not better things. We've cleaned up the air, but polluted the soul. We've split the atom, but not our prejudice. We write more, but learn less. We plan more, but accomplish less. We've learned to rush, but not to wait. We build more computers to hold more information to produce more copies than ever, but have less communication. These are the times of fast foods and slow digestion; tall men and short character; steep profits and shallow relationships. These are the times of world peace, but domestic warfare; more leisure, but less fun; more kinds of food, but less nutrition. These are days of two incomes, but more divorce; of fancier houses, but broken homes. These are days of quick trips, disposable diapers, throw-away morality, one-night stands, overweight bodies, and pills that do everything from cheer to quiet, to kill. You can choose to listen, or hit delete.[4]

BOB MOOREHEAD

Some days I was struck by how much I was changing and growing that year. Other days I wondered if I had changed at all. The day before I started teaching my English classes, I set out to buy a whiteboard marker for class. In fact, I am sure I would have bought three glistening new markers of different colors like an excited kid buying school supplies. And when they ran out, I would have thrown them away and bought more. On my way out the door, Marcelo stopped me (I was still living with his family at that point). Learning where I was going, he offered his whiteboard marker to me for use. Why would I buy a new one when there were ones that I could use? Well, honestly, because I am a rich North American who is not used to sharing. Plus, I was under the impression that the marker did not work. But then I watched him pour new ink into it and realized that he had probably been using that same whiteboard marker for years. In moments like these the reality of the economy hit me. I am used to paying for convenience in the United States, which is just not a luxury they had. He did not reuse the marker to save on waste, although that was a positive side effect. He bought ink instead of new markers out of necessity because it was cheaper, and every cut corner helped. The financial situation just forced different social norms. They placed no negative value on a car with no internal paneling or a woman who wore the same outfit for a week straight. We ate rice and drank maté because they were cheap staples. Even after all those months, it never crossed my mind to share a whiteboard marker or buy ink instead.

One night late in the year, I had a long conversation about politics and economics with a friend. He straight up asked me how much money I made in the United States. He was stunned at my salary as a private school teacher. Working with computers, cars, and farm equipment, he makes about $650 a month to support himself, his wife, and two kids. What did I do, a single woman, with over $2000 a month? We figured out that food is much cheaper in the U.S., salaries are a lot higher, and the overall standard of living is quite a bit better. He does not need to pay as much for education or health care, and was enraged at how much we were asked to spend for that. But he used the word *ugly* when realizing how I can save money while he just barely gets by month to month. And he knows with his occupation, he is doing better than most in Uruguay.

I do not tell this story to invite pity. It is good to realize that on the relativity scale, Uruguay is doing just fine. The UN comes out annually with a Human Development Index that lists 162 countries in order using the criteria of the employment rate, the average age of death, and the literacy rate. Uruguay came in at number forty-five in 2005. They have little wealth, but not much destitution either. A high percentage of citizens are getting an education and living to see adulthood. Compared to most countries in the world, they are getting basic needs met. I lived with a middle-class family in the forty-fifth healthiest economy in the world, and we reused whiteboard markers out of financial necessity. I simply cannot fathom what life would look like for a poor family in country number 162. It is time to recognize our wealth and privilege in the world. It is time to realize that billions of people are not treated like dignified human beings with inherent worth. Their basic human needs are not being met. It is time for compassion and action in our own country and in the world community.

November 19

I am having trouble with Dios. Because of my language difficulties, Dios seems like a foreign God, not my own. With the Spanish language so rigidly broken up into masculine and feminine, I feel shut down as a woman. Dios is almost always male. Jesus Christo is always Señor. So as a woman, that distances me from the Divine. I have to work so hard to get past the language barrier. I try to pray to Dios Madre y Padre, and pray that God's queendom will come, so that male images do not dominate constantly, that female qualities can rush in as an interruption and explode God to its rightful fullness. I can feel the metaphors, which never fully capture God, become saturated with female qualities, too, to become more life-giving with compassion, bearing, and nurturing. Kingdom, power, and glory need the other side for balance and wisdom and peace. Women need the cross, too, so badly here and everywhere. We are queens. We have the ability to bear life in our bodies like Christ did in death. The Church, the world needs the humble strength, the kindness, the softness of women. We need to become more visible, believe we are loved, adored, empowered to work in the world as co-creators with God and as equals to men. We are created in God's image, too, to be very good. In Christ Jesus, there is no longer male and female. We are all leveled at the cross.

May 4
   Stay silent or sound stupid? Stay silent or get laughed at? Stay silent.

May 6
   Sometimes you just grow your fingernails out so you can hang on.

November 13
   The most amazing thing happened today in small group. We were sent to talk about unity and inclusion in our social service agencies, being part of a body. I followed most of the conversation quite well, but not well enough to add anything. The group, strangers to me but friends to each other, used lingo that I did not understand, slowing me down just enough to feel like an outsider. The man next to me, who had befriended me earlier in the workshop, clued in and asked if I understood. "More or less," I said, which was the truth. I saw light bulbs go off in people's heads. They apologized and spoke with much more intentionality. The rest of the day during the large group, members of my small group took the time to approach me and make me feel visible and heard and cared for. I was used to language excluding me, so their apologies and change of behavior were fascinating to me. I experienced the gospel in action as they slowed down, noticed me, and welcomed me in as stranger. They accompanied me back into the light, into community, making it more Christ-centered, mutual, and interesting. It was powerful, and I was grateful. I only hope I can see people on the outside in my culture, and take the time to welcome them in.
   Language is so powerful. When they learn that I do not speak fluently, they think, "Who is this girl who cannot understand something that I have known for so long?" Language is alive, always changing, different in every town. Words die, and other words are born. Inflections and hand motions are unique to each spot. It is so odd for them to have to speak slowly for me. It is an interruption in their day, and it carries weight.

Bichos

You can get used to anything—haven't I already said that? Isn't that what all survivors say? [5]

YANN MARTEL

Although the determined and long-winded heat would have liked me to think otherwise, fall in Lascano officially started in March. Returning, after being gone for ten weeks, I thought for a moment I had landed in the middle of a good, old-fashioned Egyptian plague of bugs. Called *cascaduros,* these pests had taken over my town. These large, mean-spirited bugs infested us in particular because of the plethora of rice fields surrounding the town. It happens yearly, but the people said this was the worst infestation in the history of the town's consciousness. After the sun went down, it appeared that the sidewalk was black and undulating, when really it was just a thick layer of bugs meandering. They also enjoyed hovering around the streetlights and dive-bombing my head as I ran under, leaving me to pick about twenty from my hair before reaching the next light. I am not exaggerating. When I approached the safety of my home, Marina would come to the door and check me from head to toe for cascaduros, so that I would not bring any into the house. On average, she would find about fifteen that I had missed along the way. The worst part was the morning, when the town was overrun with the repulsive smell of dead bugs covering the street. The odor was invasive and persistent, as the people literally clean the bugs off the sidewalk and street with shovels. I could only hope that the frogs were not next.

Cascaduros were not the only bugs in my life. I also had to deal with my first, worst, and longest bout with lice, as I mentioned earlier. I knew it was only a matter of time, and I expected to get hit by those lovely creatures way sooner than I did. I do not know if you can have such a thing as a mild case of lice, but that is not what I had. The little guys were having a party in my head, truly "loving up" on my hair. Now, I had some very strange things happen to me in South America, but I have to admit that the lice and cascaduros creeped me out a lot more than I thought they would. I just had to accept it as part of the territory—a rite of passage, really, in Lascano.

December 18

In some cultures, moms do not swat bugs away from their children's faces because they believe that the mosquitoes are sacred messengers. I do not believe that. I think they are horrible. I woke up this morning and counted the new bites I had received in my sleep. Seventeen. Last week at the church meeting, Rosalia killed three mosquitoes on my very being. She asked me if we had bugs where I came from and said she was surprised that we suffered from bugs in our rich, "first-world country." She thought it was an annoyance reserved for "developing countries." I just smiled and let her smack another to death on my shin.

May 5
    I'm depressed. I slept for eleven hours yesterday. Lascano is winning. I cried in bed this morning, and then the vicious cycle of guilt starts: "Why can't I cut it here? My life is not hard! Suck it up!" Which just makes it worse.
    The worst part is how quickly the year stopped being about the Church, mission, learning, justice, and relationship and started being about interpersonal survival. I thought I would have a great year with the kids, make strides with the domestic violence group, and settle into the community here. They said at orientation that mission happens when expectations are replaced by reality. I just never thought the mission would be about me. I still do not know why I am here. It all seems like pointless suffering, being totally expendable, irrelevant, and useless. Why am I sitting with people who have no interest in building relationship with me?
    Here is what I do know: I, a rich, North American overachiever, have spent a year feeling invisible, silent, objectified, judged, on the outside, irrelevant, and alone. It is only a year. I am about to return to my abundant life. I already understood the power of invitation, making people be seen and heard; but I guess I have lived it now, on the other side. My sense of justice has been fed; not born, but fueled. That I do know.

April 3
    As a seminary-trained woman working at a church that does not let me do much, I wonder to myself how many gems are overlooked in the U.S. because English is not a native language. I bet there are thousands of underutilized people who are wise, resourceful, and untapped. I bet they, too, feel useless and silenced sometimes, fighting the systems.

Rubia

There is a movement to reverse the awful centrifugal force of alienation, brokenness, division, hostility and disharmony. God has set in motion a centripetal process, a moving toward harmony,

goodness, peace, and justice, a process that removes barriers. Jesus
says, "And when I am lifted up from the Earth I shall draw
everyone to myself" as he hangs from His cross with outflung
arms, thrown out to clasp all, everyone and everything, in a
cosmic embrace, so that all, everyone, everything belongs. None is
an outsider–all are insiders, all belong. There are no aliens–all
belong in the one family, God's family, the human family.[6]

DESMOND TUTU

"Ellie, will you give me your eyes?"
"Ellie, is your hair real?"
"Is everyone in the United States blonde like you?"
They had an entire year to get used to my hair, eyes, and skin color; but it just never happened. The intense attention and admiration I got for it always made me extremely uncomfortable. I often wondered where the seemingly unfounded desire to have light features came from. It made me so sad when my strikingly gorgeous and dark-featured female students actually expressed their desire to look like me. Often, when it comes to looks, different is not advisable. So why, in a sea of black hair and brown eyes, did my genes seem to be valued more highly?

On a random Friday night one of my yoga students, Mariana, invited me to her house to watch a movie. I had not watched a movie for months, and I was excited to be able to experience my students on a social level. Four of us crammed on a bed to watch a Hollywood movie with Hilary Duff called *The Perfect Man.* Did I mention these girls were seventeen? I was not anticipating that the movie would change my life in any way, but it proved to be more interesting than I had expected. First, the girls asked if it would be okay if we watched it in English with Spanish subtitles because that is what they were used to, few movies being available to them in Spanish. I started to realize then how much power Hollywood has in other parts of the world. The vast majority of movies that they watch are from my country. With this in mind, I watched the movie with a critical lens, trying to imagine what Mariana would learn about the U.S. solely from Hollywood.

This tale was about a girl who gets moved around constantly because her single mom changes cities every time a man dumps her. This single mom (Heather Locklear), not visibly receiving any financial assistance for her children, miraculously has the monetary means to pack up and drive across the country in her amazing SUV, find and fully furnish a beautiful apartment, and outfit herself and her children in the latest fashion on a cake-maker's paycheck. Hilary Duff's character, though the daughter of a single and transient baker, has perfect hair, clothes, and even her own laptop—where she narrates the movie through her blog.

I instantly thought of a single mother in Uruguay who made cakes on the side for extra money and still could never dream of owning a car, moving, or caring about fashion. A computer is definitely out of the question. Her husband died during a freak and brutal accident at work, leaving her to provide for her three kids. She vigorously cleaned houses and baked cakes, asking for help from her children constantly. The contrast between her and Locklear's character was striking, to say the least.

By the end of the movie, I had a better understanding about why my blonde hair seems to carry with it the guarantee of power, privilege, and prestige. Not only did I start making connections between Hollywood and the desire to be blonde, I instantaneously had more patience for the questions I got continuously throughout the year about my country. "Are dances in the U.S. like we see in the movies where there is a king and queen and the girls go shopping for dresses for a month?" Wince.

"Is it really true that in the U.S. the middle class is amazing? My dad said that even a pastor's family can have two cars!" Swallow hard.

"Family isn't very important there, is it? Don't you guys just rush around and skip meals like we see on television?" Deep breath.

I usually started with, "Well, it depends." Almost always, I tried with all my might to advocate for critical thinking that moves away from generalizations about an entire country, but Hollywood had ensured that I had my work cut out for me. In all honesty, sometimes when I was tired, I just agreed, because it could be so close to the truth that it hurt. Hollywood equates happiness with having things, being beautiful, and getting the boy. It has created an ideal of thin, blonde, wealthy, and carefree. This exaggerated and ungrounded ideal is being flashed all around the world. I found myself sitting on a bed with three Uruguayan teenagers who would die for Hilary Duff's cinematic life while judging their own as inferior. We do not often think of Hollywood trying to take over the world. We rarely think of the media's effect on our own brains, not to mention North American media's effect on the entire world. The messages can be subtle and subversive, but I believe Hollywood's power is one that needs to be named and thought about critically.

I believe we were all created equally in the image of God. Woman and man, God created us very good. It breaks my heart when humans ruin that by setting up hierarchies. That is why my heart hurt every time a beautiful woman in Uruguay wished for my features. Blonde hair and blue eyes and fair skin are in no way superior to dark features. Wealth and power do not make me a better person. But Hollywood is undoing what God has done. God, who sees no hierarchy but is eager to offer us all grace, loves us all irrationally. The world tries to tell us we are not all beautiful, powerful, and sacred creations. It is often easier to listen to the world than to God, who often speaks in wind and whispers while the world screams and invades. So, when I see people believing they are less than holy, I have to think of how I can add to the truth of how we are all irrevocably and radically beautiful, truly equal in the eyes of God.

December 7
I am sick of Dinorah sleeping until noon. I am sick of the Cartoon Network with horrible Spanish voiceovers distracting from the silence. I am sick of hanging on by a thread, of adjusting to a new culture, of being fat and feeling fatter, of fighting to get through each day. Today, I want to give up. I want to go home. Today is another day it will be a victory just to survive.

Comida

Bathing, dancing, praying, crying, embracing, eating—all have become acts of faith. With every running step, I praise God for the beauty of my curves that protect precious organs inside me.[7]

HEATHER SCHEIWE

During orientation in Chicago for my program, the trainers told us to talk to them before we left if we had ever suffered from things such as depression, anxiety, or eating disorders, because being far away from home and losing control over certain factors of our lives could trigger old struggles even if we were feeling strong at the moment. I thought about it, but my disordered eating from being a gymnast was so buried in my past, I thought it odd and overcautious to even consider. I did not imagine that food would be one of my biggest challenges of the year.

My struggle with food and the consequences of that struggle lasted me the entire year. Because of the slow pace of life and the high-fat, dairy diet, I gained a good amount of weight and struggled with constipation. Being a guest, I had very little control over when, what, and how much I ate. If I did not ask for seconds, the cook often was offended. The year was saturated with overeating and feeling full, bloated, and sick. When I left for Uruguay, I had been cooking an almost vegetarian diet with a marathon runner's workout schedule for seven years. Taking that away was difficult, to say the least.

I ate every part of a cow imaginable. I, with my best courage and poker face, consumed cow brain, jaw, tongue, liver, heart, kidneys, stomach lining, and intestine. I began to approach the lunch table with caution after the first day we had cow tongue as the main dish. A bowl of it sat in the middle of the table, soaked in vinegar. I could still see the taste buds. Marcelo watched me stare at his children as they enthusiastically grabbed for their portion. I swallowed hard. During lunch, I asked which part of the cow was their favorite. Two of the three said tongue. It was going to be a long year.

I started to really struggle mentally in December, more with my body than with the cow parts. I remember sitting at lunch, looking at my red pepper that had been stuffed with cheese, sitting in its own lipids and grease. The thought crossed my mind that I could throw it up. I had never thought that before. After lunch, I sat with a bloated stomach, uncomfortable, and put my entire strength into not throwing it up or thinking about the lipids absorbing through my stomach lining straight to my thighs. My demons from years ago had come back.

The next step came at Palmares during camp. I stopped eating, not completely, but enough to make a difference. I was sick of feeling fat, sick of fighting with constipation, sick of ingesting milk with animal fat sitting on the surface. No one at camp knew me well enough to notice or care. The kids were always so hungry from playing all day that I easily pushed my food off on other people, consumed energetically before other adults could catch on. I sat next to a new child at each meal, making myself invisible, as I had been the whole year. It became a game, something to keep my mind busy, my little secret. It was a goal to achieve, a way to fake being in control to make myself feel better. I wanted to go home looking different so that people would see that I had changed. I drank a lot of water to fill my stomach and looked to the kids to give me energy. I ran every day and took walks when I could in addition to all the games with the kids. I knew I was messed up and hurting. I knew it was self-destructive. But people who loved me were too far away to come and remind me who I was and that I was strong enough to eat.

After losing about fifteen pounds in Palmares, I went on family vacation with my house family. This meant losing control and eating red meat twice a day again. At one dinner, they put me on the end of the table and ceased talking to me, so the game became feeding the entirety of my dinner, at least 92 percent cow fat, to the dirty dogs that hung around the outdoor tables of the restaurant. The family concentrated on their food, animal meat lubricating their fingers and chins, thinking that I had a huge dinner. I ate nothing. I drank the table wine and made four canine friends. I was invisible.

The worst struggle I had with food started in March when I returned to Lascano. I was back to food I did not like, so fasting was easy. I did not have anyone to share meals with, so I was not missing out on the enjoyment. I got sick of myself. I could not make it inside my own head any longer. I needed to get busy, but it was not happening. My mind had nowhere to wander to. I had no one to talk to. My job, which was previously two hours a day, had not started up again after the three-month break, and that showed no signs of changing. I was looking at five months of being unemployed in a town of strangers and a family who refused to converse with me. I took to playing control games with myself, my body, and my food.

Rain always made it worse. I woke up one morning and decided not to run because it was raining, I was sick, and I had cramps. So I showered, got a cup of coffee, and retreated to my room. As I swallowed my Advil and fiber with my coffee, I got sad. It felt like I was tearing apart the lining in my stomach. I took out a notebook and started a chart of what I ate, what I did for exercise, and if my digestive track showed signs of moving so that I could tangibly on paper try to figure out the growing rolls in my stomach.

Without so much as a conscious decision, I started making myself throw up after lunch. I was not that good at it. Sometimes, I did not puke enough for it to matter; other times I just dry heaved. I was torturing myself. I am smart, so I knew exactly what I was doing. Not only was it no fun, but I also started to struggle with the self-hate of knowing how dysfunctional my actions were. I was a twenty-five-year-old woman who used to organize eating disorder awareness weeks and body image workshops in college. I just so badly wanted to have a physical consequence for the emotional turmoil that was going on. I wanted to see my hurt in the toilet, and I wanted to see my weakness in my shrinking body. It was a cry for help–to be tended to and taken seriously–to make the situation seem real. Puking meant that I was failing at this, which was embarrassing and brought self-hate. I was choosing to be a victim. I was choosing to be weak. But it also scared me enough about myself to take my situation seriously. The vomit was a tangible sign of the buried pain being unattended to. The vicious cycle wound deeper, and there was no relief.

As an alcoholic is kept from liquor, I felt like I just needed to stay away from food because I could not make intelligent decisions. I went from throwing up once a day to twice. I got better at it. I stopped thinking about it. I would starve and exercise, then break down and eat, then feel bad about it, then puke and feel better, but feel bad about that later. I kept thinking I could turn it off whenever I wanted to, but when would I want to? What damage would I cause in the process? I did not know if I should worry or whom to tell.

I thought it interesting that the one time in my life that I did not have TV, movies, media, magazines, skinny friends, skimpy clothes, bars, gymnastics leotards, or my boyfriend close to me was when I decided to throw up my food. It was not all about losing weight. It was about the boredom, the loss of control, and the lack of community to offer support in my confusion. Effects from throwing up began. My throat started to get sore, my head started to ache, and I was washed with a deep sorrow. I started to worry. At first, I thought it was about sadness, but I puked on happy days, too. So maybe it was about being heard. For months, I had been trying to start a conversation about finding a place with more work for me so that I could interact with the people of Uruguay. Conversations with my site and country supervisors had not gone anywhere, so I took initiative to speak to representatives in Chicago and Montevideo. After affirming conversations, I decided to stay in Lascano. April was too late in the year to build relationship in a new place. For better or worse, I was going to keep being present in Lascano. But I had to get out of that house. I had to start working again. I had to get busy, or I was going to make myself disappear. To give of yourself, you have to have a self to give.

I did not consciously decide to stop puking at any precise moment, but I did stop. I don't fully understand my bout with bulimia, but I know it is what forced me to be brave enough to walk away from Marcelo's house and his church to find a more life-giving situation. Marcelo's house was all that I had known, and for months leaving felt like quitting. But I finally realized that staying would have been quitting, and I chose to prioritize my health and safety first. My sickness woke me up to the reality that I was not well and needed to walk away. It shouted that I needed to take my feelings seriously. Eating became an act of faith, something that took prayer and perseverance. I decided to fight for myself, to get myself into a healthy situation. I came to grips with reality—that that year of my life was more about emotional survival and coping strategy than mission work. Sometimes the only life you can save is your own.

In my second house, I was also severely overfed, but throwing up never crossed my mind. I started working, laughing, staying busy, having outlets, and using positive coping strategies. As soon as the silence lifted, so did whatever lured me up the stairs to the bathroom after every meal. I got tired of hurting myself, I regained self-trust, self-patience, and self-love. In hindsight, it now seems to me as a time in my life that was circumstantially ungrounded, unbalanced, and unhealthy. It scares me that feeling out of control could lead me to harmful behavior, but it did. I messed with something very powerful, being fed. I rejected sustenance for a time, and then found the courage somewhere deep down to rejoin life again. I moved from that time stronger, wiser, and more alert to my weaknesses. I grew thankful for the support I gleaned from the people who showed me love, who lured me back to myself. The year was a lot about emotional survival, and learning how to eat was a part of that. The year was about letting go of control without losing a sense of who I was, and that included dealing with my changing body and struggling with my health. The year was also about accepting whatever gifts were offered and absorbing them gracefully, and that included food.

> "Help" is a prayer that is always answered. It doesn't matter how you pray—with your head bowed in silence, or crying out in grief or dancing... Some people think that God is in the details, but I have come to believe that God is in the bathroom.[8]

> ANNE LAMOTT

October 28
I am tired, so tired, sleep until August tired. I am defeated by how easily I am defeated.

> Unexpectedly, I am experiencing a deep depression...[T]he depression seems to hit me from all sides at once. I have little strength to deal with it. The most pervasive feeling is that of being an outsider, someone who doesn't have a home, who is tolerated by his surroundings but not accepted, liked but not loved... I crave personal attention and affection... The

fact that my feelings are so general and touch practically everything I see, hear, or do, shows that I am dealing with a genuine depression and not with critical observations. I have little control over it. It feels like a form of possession. I try to pray for deliverance, but prayer does not bring any relief. It even appears dark and frightening. What else can I do but wait?[9]

HENRI J. M. NOUWEN

Grace

The rabbi asked his students: "How can we determine the hour of dawn, when the night ends and the day begins?"...
"It is then," said the wise teacher, "when you can look into the face of another human being and you have enough light in you to recognize your brother or your sister. Until then it is night, and darkness is still with us."
Let us pray for light. It is the peace the world cannot give.[1]

HENRI NOUWEN

July 1

If you had told me a few months ago that my story would have a happy ending, I would not have believed you. No way. Part of me didn't want the happy ending just to avoid cliché. Part of me is glad I only will have three good months to tear away from. Part of me still thinks good is really hard. Part of me thinks it needed to happen like this. And part of me is angry that it did.

Familia

*There are things in life that we must endure which are all but
unendurable, and yet I feel that there is a great goodness. Why,
when there could have been nothing, is there something? This is a
great mystery. How, when there could have been nothing, does it
happen that there is love, kindness and beauty?*[2]

JANE KENYON

If any one person in my year was a direct gift from God, it was
Mariana. She was a seventeen-year-old youth in the church that I
first met in January. She was one of the leaders of the first camp in
Palmares, and over the course of the seven days we became friends.
She was patient with my hindered speaking and was genuinely
interested in my life.

In March when I returned from working in Argentina, no work
was available for me to do in Lascano. Mariana asked me to come
over to her house and teach her and some of her friends yoga. After
school, we would move the couch and chairs, and I would stumble
through a beginning yoga class, using my body more than my words
to communicate. She loved it, and I began to stay longer and longer
after class, having nothing else to rush off to, to talk to her and her
mom. Because of her kind questions, she figured out that I was a
bit isolated and started inviting me to do simple things like watch
a movie or have tea. Her friends became more comfortable with
communicating with me, too, and it was less and less exhausting for
them to have me around.

I could never figure out why Mariana was so kind to me. In
contrast to my home situation, it was refreshingly novel to have
someone who invited me to be me without me feeling apologetic,
without feeling judged. Where Marina shut me down, Mariana was
opening me up. One night, she asked me to spend the night at her
house, and mentioned the next day that she offered because she
sensed that my house was a difficult place for me to be.

Soon after she asked if I were able to switch homes, and her
parents approached Marcelo about it. He initially said no, that I did
not want to leave. They asked him to ask me again, and I tried to

contain my excitement at the kitchen table when he told me Mario and Julia had invited me to come live with them. A week later, when Marina was at work, I cried two tears as I said good-bye to Ignacio, knowing hanging out would disappear without sharing a house, but I instantly felt relief as I carried my travel pack across town.

The family had acquired a bunk bed and made little spaces in closets so that I could get settled in. I was told that what they had was mine to have. They asked what my favorite meals were, greeted me in the mornings, asked how my family was, and were genuinely excited to get to know me. It was shocking.

Mario was a quiet man, goodness personified. He was a mechanic who loved his family and worked hard to provide for them. He was extremely funny and showed a sensitive side just often enough to make him one of the most sincere men I have ever encountered. At age forty-eight, Julia had gone back to finish high school, and then on to law school. She traveled an hour and stayed most of the week in a dorm, returning home on the weekends to resume the role of mom. She dreamed of being a judge, which in Uruguay means she will have to move every two years so that she does not form alliances and lose her objectivity. I commended her courage and perseverance. She was very concerned that I would like her cooking, and immediately embraced me as her own. Iris, their eldest daughter, was my age, and spent the weekdays in Montevideo finishing up her studies to be a nurse. She would bring light to the house every weekend with animated stories and easy laughter. She played saxophone in a big band with her fiance, Dardo, who also played drums in a Uruguayan pop band. They invited me to events and asked me genuine questions until I felt fully comfortable in their circle of friends.

The majority of the extended family also lived in the neighborhood and excitedly absorbed me into their community. The house was much smaller, but much warmer. In the new neighborhood, doors stayed open, and neighbors were in and out all the time. My life opened up, and I inherited a dog and an unnamed cow as pets. This family lived totally differently from my first house family. Dinner was not milk, but meat. The extremes of silence and yelling at the lunch table were replaced by laughter. Family was two doors down instead of six hours away. They had no Cartoon Network and no phone. Instead of suppressing my words and emotions, this family invited them out of me enthusiastically. Instead of walking on tiptoes as to not cause a stir, I dug my heels in and relaxed. The stark contrast was jolting, in a way that would not let me wipe the smile off my face for weeks at a time. How could this family have been in Lascano the whole time without me knowing it? I knew on the first day I moved that my last three months in Lascano would not be about survival, but about grace. Getting my physical, mental, and emotional needs met by this family, I was instantly empowered to go out into the town and do mission work effectively.

Living with Mariana, I experienced a million little moments of grace. The moments hit me hard because I was so hungry for them. Sometimes, it was being in the kitchen with her while she made soup—wearing my shoes and helping me with subjunctive verb tense. Other times, she invited me into her high school, her friendships, her life. She would ask to see pictures of my family and wanted an update after each time I talked with them on the phone.

Unlike Marcelo's family, Mario's family grew up in Lascano. He and his brother, Orlando, literally built their neighborhood from scratch. So they were thrilled when given the chance to teach me about it. A few weeks after I moved in, Mariana took Tom and me to her godfather's land to go horseback riding. We were able to herd some cows, feed them, and take in the vast countryside. Galloping through the cool air, I was filled with a sense of peace. Mariana took me to soccer games, out dancing with her friends, to cultural celebrations, and to family functions. I actually felt like I was part of the community.

I started to come to life. Mariana and I went to watch Iris and Dardo at band practice, and we laughed all night. I was asked really interesting questions, not just the standard ones, and was able to engage in great conversation. I was in awe of how good this family was to me. The whole extended family welcomed me in so completely. Mauricio, the lead singer of the band said, "What a shame it took us so long to find each other, for you to find your real Uruguayan family. We are having so much fun, and you have to go soon." Wasting those months was a shame, but I felt so blessed to have this new family and relationships. Of course, I still struggled. It was hard to be cared for so much. I had very little time to be by myself. The attentiveness was almost off-putting. But I would take those struggles any day.

I decided to make a Minnesota meal for my new family, using Uruguayan food. We ate fruit during the meal instead of for dessert, drank wine, buttered bread, and stuffed peppers. They were gracious and interested. They were so animated and funny and good, so good to me. For a moment, they reminded me of my family back home.

The Allio Silvera family exceeded in three months my expectations for the whole year. They suddenly made the year about what it should have been about all along. My year stopped being about survival and started being about grace. I was nurtured and shown the country. I was welcomed into a family so that I could go out into the community and build relationships. Life instantly became safe, full, and good. Before my year, I had no space in my heart reserved for the people of Lascano. Where I once had nothing, now love, kindness, and beauty fill my heart. The Allio Silvera family filled a void. Instead of my having "people" whom I stayed with for a year, in my last three months they truly became my Uruguayan family.

May 30

I signed on to this year knowing that I would die and rise again. I welcomed the rebirth that would happen on the other side of a cross-cultural experience. I feel the Spirit awakening me. I feel Christ in me again. I think I put myself to death for a while so that I could be reborn. Now I feel it happening. I think I was dead. I think I was empty. I think I was saturated with my false self, dehydrated with my own preoccupations. The balance, the centering, the "not me" but "Christ in me" is seeping back in. I am hearing my own laughter. I am getting out of bed without a second thought. I go days without fretting. My new way of being is a mixture of who I was before and who I am now in Lascano. But, finally, I am coming to life. I am reaching out and being reached out for, thinking, reading, writing, soaking up life graciously. Finally, I am learning my new self, centered in the Spirit, not in my self-centered, false self. Finally, I know personal transformation. I have had a closed heart, but the Spirit is opening it.

Omnibus

And what of those who in their need and pain cry out to God and go on suffering? I do not know—I wish I did. Sometimes I feel all the world's pain. I only say that once. In my own need I felt a light and warm and loving touch that eased my soul and banished doubt and let me go on to the end. It is not proof—there can be none. Faith's what you find when you're alone and find you're not.[3]

TERRY ANDERSON

Traveling on the buses was one of my favorite parts of the year. It provided time to breathe, reflect, read, listen to music, daydream of home, and observe life. I would flow from intense observation to just being. Traveling alone was empowering. On the bus I realized that not a single person in the whole world knew where I was or what I was doing at that moment. I had to think on my feet, speak efficiently to strangers, and use common sense. Amidst time on the bus, it hit me that I was really living the life. I felt intensely independent *and* dependent. Simultaneously so big and so small, so alone and so engulfed, so adventurous, alive, and full of opportunity.

I would watch people get off at stops and run into the arms of their spouses, parents, and children. I cried just a bit, both missing my family and people excited to see me and also just because the world is a beautiful place full of love and welcome home kisses. Grace.

Oddly enough, one thing I was most proud of during my year is having the courage to travel across the world alone. Such courage proved a tangible example of doing something everyday that scared me. I got better at the neck pillow-sleeping upright-AdvilPM-bilingual-read to escape-watch people game. Shoes off, shoes on, passport out, chair up, belt on, coffee? Coffee? Customs form? Passport? No liquids or gels, waiting in lines, wheels, escalators, laptops, out of coffee? Up! Down! Sit, sit, sit! It was always worth it. International travel was one thing I would spend money on, marking me as a wealthy North American in an undeniable way. I always felt a mixture of invigoration, empowerment, and creativity. I write best on planes and buses when I feel both miniscule and righted in my smallness and abundantly grateful and powerful. I used to just subsist during traveling. It was a black hole for me. I would shut down something inside of me to get to the other side. But there is also value in enjoying the process, feeling how my spirit changes as the culture does. I learned to start living it, enjoying it. Now when I travel, I turn off my cell phone, buy food when I'm hungry, talk to people, pray, keep my mind turned on. It makes a big difference. I was traveling without arriving all year.

Traveling alone in South America without a cell phone at times felt like purgatory. I endured endless waiting, wondering, and worrying. I constantly faced moments of deep breathing, assessing what I was in control of, acting with common sense, and sounding completely ridiculous trying to communicate in Spanish. I have a feeling that bus stations are set up to make insecure foreigners feel like failures. You had to skip through schedules and strangers and money and fast talkers. Flat tires and delayed planes and crazy people put in the seat next to me tested me daily. No trip ever went flawlessly, so over the year, I learned to trust that, somehow, things would always work out.

I always got to my destination and always found the people I needed to find. But the pride I had to swallow in the process! Getting there, and knowing how much my North American self was challenged every time, felt like the grace of God to me. The fact that no travel situation henceforth will ever be daunting to me is a gift.

In April, travel was getting to be second nature to me, while my life in Lascano was at its worst. The trip that I was faced with at this time was not just any trip; it was Mission: Highly Possible. Rob is a man who does not sit still very well. He was getting antsy in Argentina, so he decided to come up with this mission for Tom and me. He wanted to see if he could leave the country without anyone noticing. (I would not normally recommend this to missionaries.) He sent us an outline of the mission over e-mail with agent names, responsibilities, travel cover, and a timeline. My primary responsibility, as Agent Viking, with the cover of a lost Norwegian Tourist, was to secure motor scooters, act as the leader of said motor scooter gang, and acquire munchies for Happy Hour. We would all rendezvous covertly in Colonia Sacramento at 1300 hours on April 8, undetected by all.

We accepted the mission. So I took the five-hour bus ride to Montevideo to pick up Tom, but we never found each other. I ended up waiting for him for six hours. Hiccup number one. But hiccups always built relationship, because I was always made vulnerable and had to ask people for help. In this situation, I made friends with a worker at the Internet café in the bus station, who happened to follow the Minnesota Timberwolves. I worked the kink out, bought another bus ticket, and proceeded to the said destination. On the way, I noticed turn-offs to other places I had gone during the year. I was learning the routes, as Uruguay was becoming home. No experience matches navigating myself by bus and taxi all day and opening a hostel door to familiar faces who were thrilled to see I had arrived fourteen hours after I had left my house in Lascano. The long day of waiting and travel was instantly erased as scooters were rented and driven along the ocean boulevard. I left said destination town twenty-four hours after I arrived with another eight hours of bus time in front of me, but it was totally worth it. My friends put me back together, and I let them. Mission accomplished.

Buses brought me to friends, mountains, oceans, retreats, meetings, and waterfalls. Buses taught me to live each moment, enjoying the space in the middle. Buses taught me to venture out, assert myself, be open to strangers on the journey, stay calm in inconvenience, and walk gracefully through transition. I learned more fully how to appreciate adventure and to bask in the comfort of coming home.

Vuelta

To play, to act, is to create at least a possibility of changing the world.[4]

HOWARD ZINN

Try to imagine back to the fourth grade. Just after lunch, you come in from recess and see a young substitute teacher sitting in front of the room. She looks a little timid, short, and eager to please. What is your first thought? "Fun day!"

Well, try being the substitute, with no teaching experience, in a second language, with thirty-four fourth graders thinking, "¡Qúe divertido!"

The town did not command a plethora of English speakers. I really only met one. The English teacher at the private Catholic grade school in Lascano lived over an hour away. Lascano did not have many professionals living in it. Many of the teachers who worked in my town lived in more exciting, more populated towns and took buses in and out daily. The English teacher was one of those traveling professionals; but with a sick husband and a brand new baby, she missed often.

The school found me, and put me, completely unprepared and untrained, in front of four classrooms of rowdy Spanish speaking kids who may or may not have had any interest in learning English. It went something like this: the headmaster nun, Hermana Rita, showed up at our door in full habit and asked if I could start in one hour. Some would call this baptism by fire. Others may call it a nightmare. I, being a bit of a Catholic masochist at heart and at the time feeling underworked and useless, called it a welcome challenge.

I became fascinated with the task of trying to engage these kids in learning while at times judging controlled chaos to be victory. I would leave exhausted even after good days. When I became upset and had to discipline them, the Spanish refused to flow. On several occasions I stuck my head out of the classroom and called for the headmaster, who commanded instant respect and silence upon her arrival. I did not. Daily I broke up fistfights, comforted teary-eyed kids who were being picked on, and tried to get one student to talk at a time, talk being the optimal word. With the exception of about four students, they hated to work, did not use anything less than a shout, and absolutely had no interest in staying in their seats. I looked out into the sea of kids speaking a little too fast for me to understand amidst the chaos and saw learning disabilities; emotional disorders; victims of abandonment, abuse, illiteracy, and apathy. I was supposed to teach them a skill that they would never ever need to get through life as farmers or factory workers.

I learned daily how to be a more effective teacher and convince them to get excited about English. After a Thursday that almost made me cry from the disrespect in the classroom and my seemingly failed attempt to deal with it, I walked in on Friday determined to have a better day. In each class I wrote "Flip Count" on the board. I explained that I used to do gymnastics. I told them that every time I had to ask for quiet or tell someone to return to his or her seat, the class would receive a point. If the flip count was less than ten at the end of the class, I would do a flip. To my surprise, I did four flips that day and received standing ovations from all four classes. I was an instant celebrity. I witnessed the kids sitting more attentively than I thought was humanly possible. Every time I would move a muscle to go add a tick mark to the flip count, peer pressure would squash the culprit immediately. It worked. For one day, I had their undivided attention. I walked out triumphantly, feeling twenty feet tall. The kids had been eerily respectful, and we had had a really good time working and playing with English. Oh, and did I mention that my first flip was performed undauntedly in front of the full habited headmaster nun who was observing me from the back? That is courage.

Shortly after my small victory, the English teacher quit. So every Monday, Wednesday, and Friday the flip count took effect in the second, fourth, fifth, and sixth grade classrooms in Lascano, Uruguay, because I am, indeed, a shameless English teacher who happens to be able to do a flip.

Someone once said that success is not always staying on your feet, but getting up one more time than you fall. For that one moment, I felt successful as I picked myself up one more time from a fall, earning style points in the process.

February 19

I believe in retreats, specifically ones that are a week long with best friends in the mountains of Argentina. We arrived after a twenty-hour bus ride to the mountains and lakes of Bariloche. Heaven. We sat on the rocky beach of a clear lake and took in the beauty. The water was so cold it took our breath away and shocked us into gratitude. It was a good life interruption. I just kept repeating, "We are so lucky," because I was surrounded by mountains, blue water, clear sky, and friends. God and peace were absorbing and saturating.

Last night we played cards, drank maté, and watched a movie. What fun to have a night that used to be normal in the United States and now is extraordinary! I woke to a great shower, great coffee, engulfing mountains, a hug from Andrew ten seconds after rising, and the sleepy jokes of waking friends. I am so happy I could cry. I feel so lucky, reflecting on the last two months. I have seen so much of South America, gotten to travel cheaply and experience culture.

It is nice to be in such a beautiful place so that it can comfort me and put me back together as I process difficult things. When asked about Lascano, I do not even know what to say. So much of what happens is subtle and subversive. It is hard to pinpoint and articulate without second-guessing myself and feeling paranoid. All I know is that I started crying thinking about it. The year so far has been coming to terms with the difference between my expectations and reality. I expected service to look a little bit more like work, not even productive, "tangible result"-type work, just more time to be with the kids and hang out. I have been surprised at how much of my year is being in service to the other volunteers in Argentina, and how much of it is about communicating effectively back home. Maybe my biggest role is just showing the kids of Lascano that blonde people exist. I do not regret my placement. I love those kids and wish I could interact with them more. I am thankful that I have memories that will hold me accountable when I get back home.

I feel like a player and a spectator in the first row sitting here in Bariloche. Legs dangling off the cliff, waves washing the rocky beach. The lake is alive, flowing like silk chocolate, gently with integrity. The setting sun transforms the wispy clouds in the reflection of the water. There are eighteen different blues. The mountains settled in for the long haul, furry green and wise. At a heightened state, seeking God actively, I am so happy, but not "like I could burst" happy. It is an older happiness, a weathered one. It is calm, settled, rested, alert, a deep breath sort of happy.

In a worship space that lures me into brokenness while embracing me with community and overwhelming me with God's grace, mercy, and love. Inside my own heart. I have no home now—Ombues, Dinorah's room, La Paz, Bariloche. When I cannot seek the external factors that open me up, I need to find them internally, Christ in me, peace. It is our last night here. I am bottling it up—not a frantic sucking, but a slow, trusting, knowing I will see God's beauty again soon some way. I feel infinitely lucky, comforted in my smallness, satisfied with my depth, in tune with my spirit,

in community. It has been a long week, saturated with blessings and joy—
food, laughter, nature, and conversation.

Vida Nueva

"I think about the person I used to be, and she seems so far away.
She walked fast, I walk slow. She stayed up late and got up
early, I sleep. I feel like if she gets any further away, I won't be
connected to her at all anymore."
"Do you want…to stay connected to her?"
"I think I do."
"You need to find her then."
"That's why I'm going." [5]

ANNE BRASHARES

Everything changed when I left Marcelo's house. Walking away
to take care of myself, I also walked away from being at the church's
beck and call. I stopped waiting for work, and I went and got it. After
deciding to take my own initiative when it came to work, I continued
to work for the church as much as I could. But being more present
in the town, I began to get invitations to share my knowledge until
I had built for myself a full workday. As it turns out, my two-hours-
a-day job stopped in November and never started back up again. So
it was a good decision to step away from the church and become an
independent contractor of sorts. True, it took eight months to pull
together; but with little help, I found my niche in Lascano in a way
that offered mutual relationship, sharing of lives, and a great deal of
laughter. In hindsight, I started my own one-woman ministry in a fairly
closed-off town that does not have a sense of the term "volunteer."

With no institutional support, I eventually filled a workday and
built relationships with several different communities of people in
town. A woman who works for the ELCA back home told me what
I did is usually seen in five-to-ten-year missionaries, and I did it in
one as a non-native speaker. It took me months to let go of previous
expectations, assess the situation, and act, but the end result was
not forced, and my work became more what the town wanted from
me than what I thought I would offer. That is why it worked so well.
Without preexisting institutional support, I had to break out and form
my own path: the road *never* traveled.

For an independent contractor with no contracts and no structure of any institution in particular, who is making it up as she goes, there was no such thing as a typical day. One day in May comprised: I woke at 7:30 a.m. to make a strong cup of coffee and take three stool-loosening pills for breakfast. I met Dinorah and six of her friends in the salon to teach them a dance they had asked me to choreograph for a performance they were required to do to pass music class. Three students showed up for their weekly dance class, and I wrote until lunch. Lunch was fish, eggs, noodles, and fried bananas. After the meal, I went to the preschool for gym class, where the five-year-olds started chanting my name when I came to get them and the four-year-olds gave me kisses on their way out to recess after class, all thirty-five of them. I proceeded to Mariana's for yoga and then went to my own Spanish class. I then walked to church for Bible study with the little kids, then went to the house of a woman who was preparing to travel to the United States. She gave me a cup of tea and cookies before I went into her daughter's room to teach the three girls a crash course in English. Next it was time for aerobics at the town gym, with water bottles as weights. I gave one more tutoring session to three youth group members on English so they could pass their classes. After a warm glass of milk for dinner, my sister called, and I talked to her until midnight. I no longer had time to be sad or count the minutes until I returned to the U.S. My days were so full of interactions, I could feel myself finally settle in to Lascano. By the end of the year, I was working in the preschool, grade school, high school, church, and gymnasium—as well as private homes. I knew almost every child in town by name. My English and athletic ability were most often tapped. The days became crazy, exhausting, and full. I saw it as a ministry of bodily play and laughter for the spirit. I don't think they will ever know how much the ministry ministered to me. Working within the existing systems is often ideal in mission work. But other times, the right answer can be found outside the box completely. When plan A has been put to rest, taking initiative to make plan B happen is the next step. Ideally, plan B is envisioned as much by the people as by you. Ideally, if executed, it will exceed all expectations.

March 21
　　Sometimes I wonder if I have really changed at all this year. Maybe I'm just in a holding pattern and will go back to life as usual when I return. Maybe it will be so subtle that no one will notice. Maybe it will be so much that I will be miserable. Maybe it will backfire, and I will turn

*into a mega-consumer. Maybe I will never quite know where I belong
again.*

Fiestas

*Closely related to pleasure, play is also a form of sensuousness. It
is the realm of the child, and of the child within the adult. Play
involves the ability to let the mind wander without inhibitions,
the ability to let the body be free and loose… But, "to play is
to learn to trust that the environment will not wound or maim
and to relax long enough so that one's own vulnerability can be
enjoyed."* [6]

JAMES B. NELSON

One of my favorite parts of living in another culture was observing
the different celebrations. I have already introduced you to the
annual horse breaking festival and Christmas. Another celebration
that seemed a bit foreign to me was the end-of-the-year parties in the
schools. With opposite seasons to ours, Christmas is the beginning
of their summer break. The entire town shuts down for summer. It is
often simply too hot to move at a normal pace, let alone work. The
church does not have worship in the summer because no one stays
in town. In the schools, the entire month of December is dedicated
to planning the end of the year parties–no class, no tests, just party
practice. This mainly consists of each class at every school performing
some sort of dance for the parents.

Because of my background in gymnastics, I was asked to
choreograph dances for the preschoolers and both classes in Marina's
rural school. I was able to attend the end-of-the-year performances at
the grade school. With the blind love of a proud mother, I intensely
watched the kids from the church with whom I had been working.
As I scanned the crowd (it seemed as though the entire town had
gathered), I realized how many of the children I had grown to know
and love. Spectators came up to me and said hi; the students ran to
me after their dances for hugs and encouragement. I asked all of the
kids if they passed to the next grade, which was far from a guarantee,
but most of them had.

The performances at Marina's school went really well. It was
interesting to see the families come to watch. Marina teaches six

kilometers outside of town in a one-room schoolhouse for rural kids. Among the spectators were pregnant teenagers with mismatched and torn outfits and fatigue-ridden faces. The two boys who rode horses to school every day except when it rained (because they had to stay home to help stop flooding) passed out of the sixth grade. Instead of going on, they would return to the fields full time to work. The parents watched intently and applauded energetically.

I raced from there to the preschool performances, where the club was packed with excited families. Part of the introduction was presenting me with a gift and introducing me to the spectators. All the kids were perfect. I had parents and kids coming up to me all night with kisses and gratitude. It was awesome. I had created something that had not existed there before, and, as the three-, four-, and five-year-olds jumped in hula hoops and waved their ribbons, I felt so embraced in the middle of their unabashed celebration. At first, it seemed odd to me that a month of school was spent practicing for the end-of-the-year party. But in the midst of the celebration, I got wrapped up in the excitement and joy of all the dancing and knew it was good.

May 5
Prayer changes me, how I see the world, how the Spirit flows through me, where I experience God, whether I feel lucky or not. I do not believe in the God that opens up parking spaces for me, or magically comes and transports me to another site. I do believe God is here, and I see God more often when I pray. I was praying about feeling useless and ungifted, and I think that prepared me to receive my work at the Catholic school as a gift and affirmation. I had been dreaming about making chocolate chip cookies back home, which helped me see making a chocolate cake with Mariana as a blessing. I have prayed for little things to get me through, giving me lenses to appreciate them when they were already there.

Año

While astronauts, heroes forever, spent mere hours on the moon, I have remained in this new world for [a year]. I know that my achievement is quite ordinary. I am not the only [woman] to seek [her] fortune far from home, and certainly I am not the first. Still, there are times I am bewildered by each mile I have traveled, each

*meal I have eaten, each person I have known, each room in which
I have slept. As ordinary as it all appears, there are times when it
is beyond my imagination.*

JHUMPA LAHIRI[7]

During the long, hard year, I felt every moment drip by. Living
in another culture, small moments happen less. There is less middle
ground. Things such as going to the grocery store and making a phone
call are adventures, not having the comfort of routine or knowing a
place. Challenges and joys saturated each second, as I intentionality
walked slowly and absorbed every ounce of life there. I was proud
that I survived, marveled at how I had changed, and celebrated the
excitement of my imminent return home.

I had done things I never dreamed I could do. I had traveled to
faraway places, eaten strange meals, met people who changed my
heart forever, and slept in countless different rooms around South
America. I had overcome struggles and leapt boundaries that I never
had to face before. One of the many reasons I signed on to this
program was that I was sick of being a traveler. I wanted to become
a more sensitive and responsible member of the world community
by actually living in another culture and calling it home. In this way,
my year was a success.

But a part of me felt like a cheat for walking away. With every
day I lived, I knew I was twenty-four hours closer to going home.
With every struggle I faced, I knew I could step back into life as
usual in a short while. My vulnerability, poverty, lack of power and
control, and struggle with the language and culture were temporary,
which made it easier and more comfortable in enduring it. With
that knowledge came sadness because I am privileged enough to
intentionally enter into a position of vulnerability and walk away
when I choose. Billions of people live their entire lives oppressed by
the cycle of poverty or discriminated against as foreigners without
relief. Not only did I experience relief and renewal every time I was
fortunate enough to travel with the other volunteers, I was facing
permanent relief at the end of the year. I walked in a foreigner's
shoes for a long year, but only a year. I was a relevant observer, but
on my return I became a native again. So as I struggled somewhere
between the pride of accomplishment and the guilt of temporality, I
prayed that I could continue to live a life of intentionality and service
with a newfound compassion for those who never know the relief of
power or privilege.

September 23

I am not poor. I will never be poor. If I get really sick, I would be flown to the U.S. for treatment. If I get really hungry, I can go buy more food. If I get really worn out, I can buy a bus ticket and go see the others in Argentina and stay in a hotel. I live in one of the nice houses in Lascano. Poverty is not all that I have ever known or ever will know. I just have to make it through the end of the year, and then it could, if I choose it, be over. Can I be in authentic relationship with the have nots if I have the freedom of possessions? Or if I have the option to have that freedom? I have the privilege of becoming me again in the U.S.—picking the parts I liked and analyzing why, bringing bits of Lascano with me for interest, depth, and balance…and wisdom.

June 2

I really live here. I went from my house in Lascano to the capital, on to Argentina, through the bus station to two different subway lines. I found the retreat center and got buzzed in without a second thought of what to say. I chatted with bus drivers along the way, bought food where I am a regular, and switched from bus to train without a glitch or the need to be super attentive. I live here. I love it. I did things that scared me until they stopped scaring me. I have come a long way. During the retreat, I realized that the seven of us speak and sing in both languages, appreciate food, way of life, and celebrations from both places. We talk South American politics. We share maté because we cannot live without it.

Cumpleaños

In your eyes… I am complete.[8]

PETER GABRIEL

I have many different definitions and ideas about the word *grace*. It may go something like this: Grace happens when I am offered love and joy in the time and place least expected. Grace interrupts and overwhelms with its irrationality and abundance. It is life-offering, countercultural kindness and acceptance without an ounce of earning or deserving. If there is any tidbit of truth in these ideas about grace, then on my twenty-sixth birthday, I witnessed a clinic on grace, Uruguayan style.

I spent the day of June 25 at a workshop on domestic violence that the church put on monthly to try to speak the truth in love to a town that has walked by the screaming and crying behind closed doors for years. On returning home, I found my new house family of only one month bustling about with a joyous frenzy, desperately wanting to make my Uruguayan birthday a memorable one. Goal achieved. A few hours later I entered the salon of the church to find tables full of food, dessert, and wine.

Julia had made a cake and figured out how to write "Happy Birthday" in English with *dulce de leche* frosting, my favorite. My house sister and her friends put on odd clothes, painted their faces, and performed a dance they had choreographed for me as a gift. At midnight a complete cumbia band, all friends of mine, sang "Feliz Cumpleaños." I was kissed and wished happy birthday individually by what seemed to be half the town, and laughed at as I tried to extinguish my trick candles. After a month in my new house, the family who was calling me daughter, granddaughter, niece, and sister with genuine love dropped everything to make sure I knew they were glad that I was born, that my life was worthy of being celebrated. It was grace in motion, a night I will never forget because of the laughter, music, and overflowing, irrational, and unconditional love from people I did not know existed in the world a year ago.

As if that party were not enough, it was followed the next day by another. This one was a surprise party planned and pulled off solely by the youth group of the church. Adolescents sometimes get the reputation of being self-absorbed, but this group of twenty-five spent the day baking and blowing up balloons just to see the smile on my face when I arrived. After dancing, singing, and laughing for a few hours, about half of the kids biked alongside of me, accompanying me as I walked all the way home. The generosity of kids was then seconded on Monday, when my fifth graders blindfolded me with my scarf (my first June birthday with winter gear) and led me to the school chapel where I was bombarded with flowers, balloons, and cards in both English and Spanish. Again, without any prompting from parents, these kids had scurried around all day to make sure I was wrapped up in love and affection on my birthday.

Sometimes I wondered who was teaching and who was learning. What did I do to deserve this? Nothing. That is the beauty of it. That is why it is grace. I was left to humbly and graciously say thank you, accepting countless hugs, kisses, and little Uruguayan trinkets. There is a time to give and a time to receive. I only hope I was able to offer a glimpse of the love, acceptance, and grace back before I left.

My older sister from home sent me the best gift. In her card she wrote to me that the best gift I could give myself was grace as I leave

Lascano. She knew I had been hard on myself, feeling guilty for not thriving and giving more. I gave it my best shot, trying to forgive myself and be patient, letting myself be proud for the little that I did and realizing that what I did was not even the point. It felt good to realize that I had already learned to accept the grace offered to me daily. I did what I came to do, to be a relevant observer and go back to the most powerful country in the world changed, transformed by love.

March 24

I think I have grown up a lot this year. It crept up on me. For as long as I can remember, I have hated things like grocery shopping, laundry, or going to buy, I don't know, batteries. These are all fairly necessary things in the whole scheme of life, but they felt like a waste of time for me because they in no way contributed to me saving the world. I could not see how they were really beneficial in my plight to rid the world of injustice, and it just took precious time away from that plight. Why go buy shampoo when I could be writing an essay or sitting on a committee or giving advice to a friend over a beer? But this year, oddly, when I dream of the United States, I have not been dreaming of essays and committees. I dream of going to the market and spending hours on a Saturday making a great meal while sipping wine and listening to good—really good—music. I think that nothing sounds better than curling up in my apartment with a book on a Sunday (after church of course) while waiting to change loads of laundry. I think it sounds so romantic to have a day totally on my own when no one knows where I am, picking out paint for the bathroom and stopping to buy a coffee (at the local shop with my reusable mug) to keep me company.

I don't want the false idea of greatness and power I once did. The weird, overly ambitious striving has left me, maybe temporarily, but maybe for good. I am dreaming of normalcy, of celebrating little things in life, the calm of self-knowledge and confidence. I think I have learned what is really important, and sometimes that is taking care of myself and knowing the world will not end because of it. No, spending two hours in a bubble bath painting my toenails purple after dusting the living room won't stop world hunger or strengthen that friendship that is slipping away. It won't bring prestige or a bigger paycheck. But now I can see the value and goodness in it. And these are the moments I dream of.

These are the moments I work to make available for everyone. We all deserve leisure time, the opportunity to have choice, the luxury of thinking about something or nothing because we are not paralyzed thinking about survival. So many people do not have that. They are so rightly occupied with where meals are and hotel vouchers and school supplies and which buses will get them there. Stability, normalcy, the absence of fear, the freedom of choice should be available to us all. These things should come with justice and equality. We are not there yet, which is why I will get out of the tub with my purple toenails and go to that committee meeting until it happens.

Carachas

Galaxies revolve and dinosaurs breed and rain falls and people fall in love and uncles smoke cheap cigars and people lose their jobs and we all die—all for our good, the finished product, God's work of art, the Kingdom of heaven. There's nothing outside heaven except hell. Earth is not outside heaven; it is heaven's workshop, heaven's womb.[9]

PETER KREEFT

Now, I am not brave enough to venture any guesses about what heaven may be like, but I really hope it has waterfalls. With other volunteers whom I did not know a year ago and now call amazing friends, in July I ventured to a paradise on earth where Argentina, Brazil, and Paraguay meet. This was the last time I would go back to Lascano after a trip. Only a month remained. We spent two marvelous days hiking around the National Parks of Iguazú. Before this trip, I was never able to lift up two neighboring days and say with such gumption, "Because of those two days of my life, I am a better person." I stood in a hushed silence with my feet in cool water, the warm sun on my hair, drinking in the beauty of mossy rock and roaring water. I had no inclination to move or act or do or talk. Being in the presence of that much beauty overwhelmed me with goodness, love, and all that is peaceful and right.

By this point in the year, the silence of Marcelo's home and the oddity of having nothing to do for months was a memory. It was fresh, but it was a memory. I had Mario's house and lots of wonderful kids at work to return to. But I needed those two days for restoration. My heart changed and healed. I wanted to be alone, and I wanted everyone I have ever loved or ever will love to be with me all at the same time. I took in a deep breath of fresh air; and before I could let it out, two tears calmly spilled over my lids as if I was so full that something needed to maintain the homeostasis so I would not burst. I cried because I had to leave South America. I cried because I would get to go back to the United States. I cried knowing that my kids in Lascano will never get to see something so beautiful and restoring. I cried because it was so invigorating, and I am so lucky. I cried because I felt so small and the world felt so big, which I found wonderfully liberating.

Sometimes we walked the trails alone, savoring moments full of our own thoughts and feelings. Sometimes we laughed and reflected together, snapping pictures, pointing out exotic birds, and rubbing elbows at the overlooks. The sight, smell, and sound of rushing water mesmerized and awed us. Convinced it could not get any more beautiful, we found that around each bend the waterfalls took our breath away again. Andrew approached me at one overlook, pointed to a small trickle of water across the way, and said, "God loves that waterfall, too." Yards away from powerful bursts of water, I connected with the tiny, yet visible trickle and choked back a tear in the truth of his statement. At another overlook, it was too loud to talk. I found myself screaming in delight like a little girl as the massive waterfall just feet away drenched me. We watched some waterfalls for minutes and others for what seemed to be an hour. It never got old. The water cleansed us, renewed us, entertained and comforted us.

Our days were spent among the waterfalls, our nights with good food, wine, and conversation. We spoke about how the waterfalls are not an attraction that shuts off at 5 p.m. and starts back up at 9 a.m. for tourists. Even while we slept, the soft, cool, refreshing water glided over old, stubborn stones, carving them with patient, persistent presence. The noise was powerful and soothing. Something about that placed changed me, healed me, gave me new hope.

Those waterfalls were a sacred place for me. My friend Courtney– who had died before I left–had a butterfly tattooed on her foot. When I encountered butterflies in Uruguay, I felt a bit more connected to her. The park was overrun with butterflies of all different colors and sizes. Our second day at the park was her birthday, and I felt close to her there in a way I had not yet felt in her absence. I experienced God the Creator in a whole new way for two days continuously. Without thinking, I whispered, "I love you," into the abyss. I felt the answer inside of me and was awed that a small piece of the same beauty that surrounded me could exist in me.

December 10
    The thing about making myself so raw and needy is that I would go out into the world desperate to get my needs met. I saw grace in places I had not noticed before because I was actively seeking out grace as a survival skill. So many nights I would cry for hours, clinging to certain song lyrics as a lifeline: "This is the one thing I know. You said you won't let me go."[10] *When I woke in the morning, still alive, I would go out on the streets so hungry for love that I would actually find it in places I would overlook in the U.S. when I felt put together and self-sufficient. Kisses from preschoolers, pictures drawn for me by my students, a friend picking up my call even if the number came up as unavailable, the old woman on the corner stopping me to chat, these things literally held me up. I could clearly and tangibly feel them sustaining me. Grace was all around, and I could finally see it. It was either appreciate it or perish. The fog lifts. God answers. The simplicity of it is breathtaking.*

Corredor

And maybe it is only on the trail to nowhere-in-particular that you find the most important thing of all. Yourself.[11]

DOUGLAS WOOD

Running in the fields gave me hope, so I ran almost every day. I enjoyed alone time to think and clear my head and be active. It reminded me that if nothing else, I was not, in fact, paralyzed. Some days it was enough to put one foot in front of the other, to move because I could. I prayed that somehow that movement contributed to life until a brighter day. On some really hard days, the cosmos mourned with me, and it started to rain. Running in the rain was always cleansing. The cold snapped a little bit out of me, and for once I felt tough and strong. The paved routes didn't talk back. The pavement didn't care how angry I was or how hard or softly I chose to pound on it. The pavement didn't try to ask questions or try to make me feel better. But it was always there—predictable, dependable, consistent. My heart beat, my blood flowed, my legs moved, I focused past the raindrops while letting them wash me. That was enough. That was healing.

On my favorite loop, the end of the run took me downhill into town. I could see for kilometers ahead. I always took a moment at the top of the hill to take in the beauty. My heart felt light, and the fields stretching out made me feel so small. It made the world seem big and beautiful, with a power and spirit all its own. It put me in a place in the cosmos, small, but connected to all that was before me and all that is to come. It reoriented God for me. I was not small in a degrading way; rather, it empowered me and freed me to do what I could—no more and no less. God is God and I am not, but I am loved by God and connected to that God and the cosmos. I am small, but strong, filled with peace.

As I started downhill, I took in the long phone lines running out of town. Cows and phone lines. I became grateful for the phone lines that miraculously brought voices of people I love to me in that faraway place. It felt as if someone built all those phone lines between Lascano and Minnesota so that I could be in love, so that I could be sustained.

My favorite time to run was during a sunset. It was comforting to know that there will be a sunset every night while I am alive on earth. With no buildings in the way, the sunsets were better than art, better than movies. They filled me up with beauty, quieted me with awe. Every night the show was different, but equally awesome. The show was free. It was pure grace—God's creativity. God never seems to get sick of color and beauty and movement and goodness. Each sunset is different, a gift that instantly brings oozing peace and abrupt awe. Oranges and pinks confidently splashed against blues, dancing behind tin rooftops and palm trees. I saw the sun set over the ocean, the rivers, while riding on a bus by myself, and on my roof. But my favorite place to watch it was at the top of the hill on my run. It filled me up as I headed back home.

Running is for rich people. The people looked at me as if I were crazy. How strange, that North American girl who runs just for fun! Wouldn't it be nice to have such an easy life that we had to seek out activity? In Lascano, where much of the work was in the cow field and the rice factory, everyday life offered time for reflection, and hard work kept the body busy. In the United States in my experience, I fight for time for myself and strive constantly for fitness and balance. So, though I felt bad running every day like a crazy person, I was used to more movement in my life than they were giving me, so I had to go get it. I would have risen to the challenge of working the fields from dawn to dusk. But, instead, my lack of workload caused me to sit and get anxious. So running became my therapy, and I understood that it was a luxury that not all people could enjoy.

October 5
There are no big victories here for me. I'd like to think that I
appreciated small victories in the United States, but I live for them here.
I cherish them. That is all that I have. They change my life. They show
me grace. They get me through my day. They are my daily bread. Maybe
because life is slow here, I am being patient with myself. The small
victories are enough. I will get to where I need to be in time. It is okay for
me to be totally present with my thoughts and a cup of coffee in an empty
house in front of the fire in Lascano, Uruguay.

Victoria

Be not afraid of growing slowly. Be only afraid of standing still.

CHINESE PROVERB

If I had made a list of life successes in the United States, it would
have included things like awards won, marathons finished, and high
test scores. In Uruguay, my definition of success changed. This is what
I came up with for why my year in Uruguay was a success:

I laughed more than I cried.

I won the affection of preschoolers.

I did things that scared me everyday.

I learned how to gracefully fail and laugh at myself.

I learned that the world is big and does not revolve around me.

I became bilingual and bicultural.

People who used to be random Uruguayan citizens I now call
friends.

I tangibly experienced the sustaining power of prayer.

I traveled around a continent by myself using a second language.

I learned to knit, play the guitar, ride a scooter, eat odd parts of a
cow with a game face…

I was awed into a peaceful silence by mountains, oceans, and cow
fields full of stars.

I wore only two pair of pants all year.

I realized that I am human and became gifted at naming my needs
and getting them met.

I survived lice, mange, fleas, and countless digestive problems.

I came to believe that my worth does not, indeed, depend on my
productivity.

I listened more than I spoke.

I taught Ignacio how to tie his shoes and blow bubbles with gum.

I introduced Frisbees and peanut butter to the people of Lascano.

I got reacquainted with my smell without deodorant, my hair without product, my face without makeup, and my legs without shaving.

I like this list better. These are not what I anticipated would be my big accomplishments, but now that I have lived to the other side, they are things that I am deeply proud of.

June 7

I am going to miss all the kids in town knowing my name, Mariana lifting my spirits with her silliness after a long day, seeing four people on a moped or three on a bike, wheels used as plant potters, the energy of the youth, the amazing sunsets and stars, and people being nice to me for no reason. I leave a place without many roses to stop and smell, but they have unbelievable sunsets to watch! I look up, but I also look down. The torn-up streets and sidewalks will always be legendary.

I love when Facundo proudly tells me that it is his birthday. I love when I run into Walter and Federico on the street and encourage them to come to youth group. I love when I see one of my fifth grade students biking with her preschool brother sitting in her basket, both screaming my name and waving. I love when I wave at the truck drivers, and they wave back, when my English students finally get it, and when I can see the "aha" moment cross their faces as they smile and begin to get excited and hopefully see the world differently because for one moment they believe that they are smart. I love taking roll call and laughing with the students at my horrible pronunciation. I have finally figured out that I am not here to teach English or dance or aerobics or gym. I am here to hang out with kids, and the classes are just an excuse to do so. I have finally figured out how to be active, to fight being a victim, being invisible, being objectified. As nice as invitations are, it works better to be active and make sure that people know that I am human. We are all in the occupation of planting seeds, and rarely do we get to benefit from the harvest, or even know that it happens. But sometimes, I walk into a group of kids in town and realize that I know them all. I realize walking away, after asking them all questions and giving them kisses, that I have come to know and love a town of people. I have beautiful relationships that have formed before my eyes over the year, a bountiful harvest.

Adios

Time tells the truth.

FROM A FORTUNE COOKIE

When my year in Uruguay was complete, my second house family came with me to the bus stop to see me off. As I turned the corner, the first face I saw was that of a beautiful three-year-old named Juliana, who used to be a random child across the world, but whom over the year I had grown to love and call a friend. I was Juliana's gym teacher in preschool even before I moved into the house next door to hers late in the year. She is gorgeous, and quickly became one of my favorites. I began to sob, not knowing if I would ever see her again, not knowing if she would remember me if I did.

Her face was followed by dozens of others who had, to my surprise, taken a break in their day to come say good-bye. It was so overwhelming. What a bittersweet ending. This, indeed, is not a tragedy. This could only happen in a small town. Somehow, in a few short months, a town in Uruguay had come to embrace me and I them. I fell in love with an entire village of people. And they all showed up at the bus stop that day to wish me well. I continued to sob as I hugged them, one by precious one. This, also, could only happen in a small town.

The bus started its five-hour journey to Montevideo from my town a bit late. I had come to know the bus drivers well, so they easily overlooked the departure time, and let me say good-bye to each person. There were women from the gym, kids from the school, elders from the church, family, and friends. Dardo, who said he did not cry ever, had tears streaming down his face. Mariana, the most near and dear of my friends, my first real advocate, tried to make jokes but ended up breaking down with me. My first house family did not cry, but they did show up, all but Marina. I was handed gifts, pictures, and cards. I was touched, smiled at, and reminded that I always had a home and family there to return to. After two steps up the bus's stairs, I turned back to give a final smile and wave, looking deeply into the sea of faces that had held me and taught me so much and took a snapshot in my mind that I will cherish forever.

I found a seat in the all-too-familiar bus, and put a sign up in the window that read, "Ya Extraño." I already miss you. And I smiled and waved through the tears that I had not known were in me.

As the bus pulled away, most of the people started running across the plaza. I watched them run, having no idea what was going on, which was a theme to the year I had grown comfortable with. On the other side of the plaza as the bus pulled around, they began to form a human chain in the street and started chanting, "¡Ellie no se va, Ellie no se va!" Ellie can't go. The bus slowed, and they clung to each other. They did not want me to stay because of my competency. We had grown to love each other just by being. The bus driver, my friend, turned gently and asked, "What do you want me to do?" I thought it was time to go home. It was a day I had been dreaming of fondly all year. But now that it was here, the idea of home was becoming quite fuzzy. Luckily, I did not have to answer the bus driver's question. The mock rebellion over, the chain disbanded and its links waved fervently as the bus drove out of town.

Some people were not part of the chain. These people had raced ahead so I would have familiar faces encouraging me down the road until we turned at the route and headed for the capital. The last faces I saw belonged to the most beautiful children in the entire world: Ignacio, Santiago, and Dinorah, my first house siblings.

I will carry all these people with me always. They showered me with God's grace until I believed it to be true. I lived with them and grew to love them. And that was enough for them. They gave me more than I deserved, more than I earned every day. They forgave me for my North Americanness and loved me, not because of my success or ability, but simply because I am human. I lived slowly enough to allow Uruguay to seep into my blood. The people crawled into my heart. The culture saturated my soul. As the bus drove away, I thought, "There is a time to give and a time to receive. I only hope I have been able to offer, in return, the smallest reflection of the love, acceptance, and grace I have been offered here." I knew that the day I returned to the United States was the day I would begin work. It was time to tell the story. My story. My beautiful story. It was time to share the transformational Uruguayan adventures of a rich North American overachiever.

> Life is this simple. We are living in a world that is absolutely transparent, and God is shining through it all the time. This is not just a fable or a nice story. It is true. If we abandon ourselves to God and forget ourselves, we see it sometimes, and we see it maybe frequently. God shows Himself everywhere, in everything–in people and in things and in nature and in events. It becomes very obvious that God is

everywhere and in everything and we cannot be without Him. It's impossible. The only thing is that we don't see it.[12]

THOMAS MERTON

Epilogue

There is nothing like returning to a place that remains unchanged to find the ways in which you yourself have altered.[1]

NELSON MANDELA

It took a whole year to feel at home again in the United States. I was out of sorts, different, changed. I had lost my ambition, my sense of self. I was disillusioned and scared and very, very sad. I went to therapy to deal with completely losing my sense of vocation for the first time in my life. I distanced myself from Uruguay to survive, not writing or calling as much as I wanted to or thought I would. I felt utterly homeless, alone, confused, and tired at my core.

I overworked myself, but not at things that brought me fulfillment. I had a lot of self- hate, not knowing who I should be, not knowing why I could not return to the likable workaholic I used to be, liking the pre-Uruguayan Ellie better than the one I had become. I could not muster the energy to call friends, to try. I cried. A lot. I went into survival mode.

I broke up with Dan to try to make it all less complicated. I became infantile and selfish so that I could function. I did not know how to hold on to Uruguay and be fully present in the United States all at the same time. I did what a good type A overachieving North American would do: made a list. I joined a gym. I stopped eating meat. I found work, drew, wrote, cried, and slept. My therapist put words to what I was feeling. She told me I talked like people who had been through experiences of solitary confinement. I was overstimulated. Uruguay slowed me down and changed my life. So, with her blessing, I stopped feeling guilty for doing what my body wanted to do: after work, I would come home, turn the lights down, and be very, very alone. I lit candles, watched mindless television, just sat, sometimes waiting for it all to pass and sometimes actively processing through the emotions. Honoring the desire to be alone and be quiet after a full day of work made sense. My friends would have to be patient. I had to put myself back together.

The sixty-seven young adult volunteers from the program that year had a retreat together to talk about the reentry process. It was quite validating. The experienced leaders advised us not to make any big life changes for a year. It was sound advice. I worked a job, but it was not a career. I lived with my sister, who laughed me back to life. I let myself off the hook and just let myself settle back in for a year. For the second year in a row, I was patient with myself. I spent a lot of time with Tom, Andrew, Alyson, and Christine, who had all moved back to Minneapolis. I told different versions of my story to different audiences, and I got more solid footing in the U.S.

Then, as if a switch had flipped, I came back. It took a year of my life, but I did come back. I found work teaching theology in a community that gives me life and offers me love. I asked Dan to come back to me, and he graciously did. After a year a hemisphere apart, we went on dates and learned how to have fun together again. Shortly after the year mark, it became abundantly clear that Dan was the most amazing, generous, calm, good-to-the-core companion I could ever dream of. I asked him to be my partner for life, and he said yes.

Fifteen months after I had gotten on a plane to go home, I got back on a plane to Uruguay to see Iris and Dardo get married. When I bought the ticket with mixed emotions lodged in my trachea, I had no idea I would be going, in part, to write the epilogue to my story. The day I packed my suitcase to return to Uruguay, I signed a book contract. People I've never met before would come to know Orlando, Julie, Mariana, and Maria José through my story.

I put wedding planning, book writing, gymnastics coaching, and teenager teaching on hold. I left my affluent life, fancy clothes, and laptop to eat cow, drink tea, and sit with people across the world whom I love. I dusted off the journal that had not been touched in fifteen months. Why had I not written much in the United States? Maybe because I was with people all the time, speaking in English, comfortable, trying to live the contrast, finding joy in my North American life. It felt so different than the first time I flew out. This second time, I was leaving home to go see my other *family*. There would be no pacing myself, no survival tactics. There was no unknown; it was vacation.

I woke up after a deep, Advil PM-induced sleep, in another world. Argentine fashion, Spanish spoken around every corner, Hasidic Jews in the smoke room, old ladies in heels adorned with gold, duty free shopping. I started crying in the bathroom of the airport. Countless memories came flooding back as I took in the thin toilet paper, the Spanish-influenced tiling, the subtlety of different locks, flushes, handles, and a sink that I associate with a different hemisphere, country, people, and life. Men unashamedly check out women. Rooms are filled with loud, spirited political conversation. I grew emotional as it hit me that Mariana would be on the other side of the next flight, waiting for me.

And she was. Mario had borrowed a truck from a friend, took the day off work, which is a big sacrifice for him, and drove his wife and daughter hours just to be there when I came in. The Spanish started off rocky, but quickly came back. I changed $50 into Uruguayan pesos that I was not allowed to spend a dime of. The generosity of these people is mind-boggling.

Juliana, the three-year-old who had started my sob session at the bus stop the day I left, is five now, but she did not forget who I was. When I walked past her house upon arriving back in Lascano, she was outside. Taller, with longer dark curls, she gave me the greatest gift–the look and smile of recognition and excitement. She ran toward me with arms outstretched to give me a kiss as if no time had passed. Not all the kids cared that I had come back, but she did. Grace personified. Later that day when I was next door taking maté with the relatives, she walked across the yard a number of times to give me different drawings she had made. The next day, she would sit on my lap at the wedding. It was good.

Everyone I encountered offered me a spirited kiss on the cheek, asked how my family was, and told me how skinny I had gotten. The tiny interactions that reminded me of the goodness of the people made me miss my simple, rural life. Walking everywhere by way of the middle of the gravel roads, the hot sun beating down, dogs running free, and a familiar face around every corner encapsulated the year and brought it all back.

With hindsight comes so much wisdom. What a gift that I could go back! The trip was a microcosm of the year that I spent there. My time was so short that I could not do everything and see everyone. I had to choose well. I chose to accompany my family during the wedding festival. I watched them work like dogs to prepare for the celebration–clean the church, carry freezers, chop wood, make drinks, cut flowers, but I did not feel bad watching and taking it all in like I used to before. It was not about me. There is so much freedom in that. They gracefully took me in and let me participate. I helped when I could, not being as productive or efficient, but that was not the point. I walked with them from beginning to end, often with my mouth shut, my arms full, and my eyes and heart open.

I resisted the urge to bring a gift. I finally let them teach me that despite my disbelief in myself, my presence is the best gift I can give, even when I seem to add little and take much. The big and little moments that make life—those five days were full of both, full to overflowing. I walked around town without feeling odd or sad. I made mistakes with my Spanish without being embarrassed or shutting down. I never lost the feeling, in every moment of those five days, that I had a home and a family there. It is not where I come from or where I am going, but it is a part of who I am.

When it was time for the wedding to start, I forgot for a moment that I was in South America. Here is how it went down. After two days of prepping the church and reception site, and I mean we did *everything*—picked every flower, sewed the dresses, moved tables, made decorations, everything—we sat and relaxed in the afternoon sipping maté. The wedding was scheduled to start at 9:30 p.m., and no one was moving at 7:00. They had one shower to accommodate the entire extended family, who would later sleep anywhere they could fit. At 9 p.m., I was reading and waiting, curiously watching the house turn into a three-ring circus. At 9:25, five minutes before game time, I was amusedly gazing at Mariana, who was having her hair done leisurely—no make-up, no dress. In walks the groom, and I began to settle down. They would not start without him. He looked great in a suit, was totally calm, and I laughed as pure chaos ensued. We probably got to the church, which was already becoming packed, about fifteen minutes late, which was indeed early. An hour later, the bride showed up, and the ceremony began. People were standing in every available inch, spilling over to outside all the way to the street. After Iris and Mario walked down the isle, people filed in after them to get a better look. The ceremony included two songs, an efficient sermon, exchange of rings, a kiss, and we were on our way to celebrate.

The party began with an hour of sandwiches, any combination of whiskey, coke, and beer one could imagine, and joyful chatter. The dancing began at 1 a.m. and lasted until 8 a.m., pausing only for a dinner of salads, chorizo, and asado around 3 a.m. and the cutting of the cake an hour later. When the party was in full swing, *tambores* players entered as we passed out large, colorful hats, ties, and plastic maracas while silly string was shot into the night. We danced until the sun came up and then some. It was a rite of passage of sorts. To become a member of this group of people, one must dance one's heart out until all hours of the morning. The Uruguayans know how to celebrate. I danced with all the men of my "family," and they all knew how to dance very well. I laughed with all the women, played with all the kids, and ate with all the grandparents. Almost every person I had come to know and love while in Uruguay was in one place, loving each other and loving life. It was as if I could hear every heartbeat in the room.

Some moments in life are so full to overflowing that time itself seems to stop. The space becomes thin, the joy mixes up all of the senses, and one seems to float, hover, glide through space with delight and ease, meeting no resistance. This was one of those moments.

I walked home by myself at 8 a.m. and slept on the floor around extended house family members until 11 a.m. As my heels worked through the gravel, oddly dressed up for the time and place, I could not wipe the smile off my face. It was a good day. I felt so blessed to be able to come back and celebrate with these people who had become my family. As I took maté and ate lunch with the family, people swung by to say good-bye and thanked me for coming. My heart sank a bit as the borrowed truck pulled up, signaling time to head for the capital to get my flight. I started to shake and cry while putting my stuff together, and gave hugs and kisses all around. People told me to come back when I could, one uncle reminding me that caskets do not have pockets to hold money. The groom sincerely thanked me for my presence, knowing it is not easy or cheap to come, and he bid me well in *my* planning, saying, "Now, it is your turn." My houseparents did not cry at the airport, and neither did I. They reminded me that I have a home and family there always, and that I should come back when I can.

The trip was pure goodness. I experienced no culture shock the second time. My Spanish was fine. I spent a good time with my family there. I can't help but think that life would have been easier, neater, if I had never ventured to Uruguay the first time. I would have had a clearer sense of where home was, who family was, a less complex view of the world, less internal conflict when spending money or voting or choosing a job. On the plane back, thinking of how one day I was in the sun eating asado and laughing in Spanish, and a day later would be teaching theology in a turtleneck sweater was almost too much to carry. The rest of my life will be different because of Lascano, Uruguay. Faith is not about clarity. Love is not neat. Faith is about relishing, thriving in the muckiness of love.

How can one person be so blessed? I have two homes, two lives, two families, and two cultures. I speak two languages, love two communities of people, and I am called to honor both fully with my whole heart without compartmentalizing. If nowhere else in the world, Lascano, Uruguay, and St. Paul, Minnesota, overlap and interact in my very being. I praise God for the growing capacity in my heart to hold both realities—with all the pain and joy, contradiction and friction, disillusionment and discussion—with grace and the weight of being a bridge builder.

This is not the end of the story. But whatever is to come, I can safely say it is a story worth telling over and over.

Nothing we do is complete, which is another way of saying that the Kingdom always lies beyond us. No statement says all that should be said. No prayer fully expresses our faith. No confession brings wholeness. No program accomplishes the church's mission. No set of goals and objectives includes everything.

This is what we are about. We plant the seeds that one day will grow. We water seeds already planted, knowing that they hold future promise. We lay foundations that will need further development. We provide yeast that produces effects far beyond our capabilities. We cannot do everything, and there is a sense of liberation in realizing that. This enables us to do something, and to do it very well.

It may be incomplete, but it is a beginning, a step along the way, an opportunity for the Lord's grace to enter and do the rest.

We may never see the end results, but that is the difference between the master builders and the worker. We are the workers, not the master builders; ministers, not messiahs. We are prophets of a future that is not our own.[2]

ARCHBISHOP OSCAR ROMERO

Teología

*We will have to repent in this generation not merely for the
vitriolic words and actions of the bad people, but for the appalling
silence of the good people. We must come to see that human
progress never rolls in on the wheels of inevitability. It comes
through the tireless efforts and persistent work of men [sic] willing
to be co-workers with God...*

   *Whenever the early Christians entered a town, the power
structure got disturbed and immediately sought to convict them for
being "disturbers of the peace" and "outside agitators." But they
went on with the conviction that they were "a colony of heaven,"
and had to obey God rather than man [sic]. They were small in
number but big in commitment. They were too God-intoxicated
to be "astronomically intimidated." They brought an end to such
ancient evils as infanticide and gladiatorial contest.*

   *Things are different now. The contemporary church is often
a weak, ineffectual voice with an uncertain sound. It is so often
the arch-supporter of the status quo. Far from being disturbed
by the presence of the church, the power structure of the average
community is consoled by the church's silent and often vocal
sanction of things as they are.*[3]

MARTIN LUTHER KING JR.

I sat at orientation before leaving the United States, listening to a
series of lectures by people who lived and taught the mission theology
of the ELCA's Young Adults in Global Missions program. I quickly
became an excited student, taking notes and coming alive, realizing
that I had made a wise choice in program. No matter how hard the
experience of living in a new culture was going to turn out to be, I
believed in what I was doing, and the theory that held me up. I got
the sense that God was calling me to be a relevant observer in the
world, to be lucky enough to witness transformation and restoration
in an interesting community away from home.

Rafael Malpica-Padilla, the Director of the Global Missions
department, spoke of how the community I was about to enter would
legitimize *me,* not the other way around. That legitimization would be
a gift and must be earned through relationships. The world is full of
broken community. Communities struggle with violence, poverty, and
diversity—the communities we came from and the ones we were going
to. He encouraged us to go, be present, and become parts of these

new communities. After a year, a bond not there before would form between people across the world and me. He cautioned us to keep in check the desire to have the people we encounter become more like us, instead seeking to notice similarities and be open to learning and changing because of what we experience. It was not my goal to turn Uruguay into the United States. I was hoping to bring a piece of Uruguay back with me. I did not need to become them, but I did need to eat their food when it was offered, sleep in their homes, and let the Spirit break down barriers that humans have built up.

I had never thought about how my life and lives in Uruguay were connected, but I was going to see with my own eyes. Before the year, thinking of the people in Uruguay, all I felt was disconnect and difference. Maybe we were so different that they would have nothing to teach me.

Beginning during that orientation in Chicago, I continuously remembered that God was already working in Lascano. I prayed fervently at night for a spirit of humility, compassion, respect, hospitality, mutuality, and solidarity. I begged God to open my eyes, that I might see God in each person and in the different language, lifestyle, food, faith, tradition, life experience, ethics, and clothing. I prayed to be equipped with strength, welcoming the possibility that opening my heart up to the pain of others would change me in a way that I would feel for the rest of my life. I imagined that emptying myself of stereotypes, pride, superficiality, and suspicion would be emotionally exhausting, but essential. I began to realize that being a missionary would ask me to both observe and participate, listen and speak, share suffering and share joys, receive and give, learn and teach, build community and empower builders, be a witness and be witnessed to, be healed and heal, and—more than anything—allow myself to be transformed.

Looking back, this is what happened. Those feelings during orientation in Chicago came to be. I have come back more whole. I have come back transformed. And I do believe that the people in Lascano who offered me love feel the same. What I learned there was that I am not an isolated woman from the United States. I am intimately a part of a global community. I came back more complete because I had lived with these people. On a macro scale, I believe that the United States will become more interesting, more whole, as we continue to recognize our connections to people across the world.

I believe that God loves me radically. That love is liberating. As a free North American with power and privilege, I can move into contact with my neighbor. I can love God by loving my neighbor, and that neighbor does not need to live next door. God anointed David, the youngest, as king. Abraham was unexpectedly chosen; God came to a peasant woman, Mary, to become flesh; and Jesus died as a slave on the cross. Our faith is about hierarchy being abolished. There is no longer man or woman, slave or free, Uruguayan or American. We are all created lovingly in the image of God. God's vision of community includes no outcasts, for we have all been called to God in a loving embrace through Jesus' outstretched arms on the cross. We face no boundaries, no country lines. The world does not yet reflect heaven. We get glimpses, but God calls us to be co-creators on earth, to usher in holiness, to erase boundaries, to laugh and break bread and transform and dance together, so that God's community comes to here and now.

Notes

Preface

[1]Aboriginal Activists Group, Queensland, 1970s.

[2]Ann Brashares, *Sisterhood of the Traveling Pants* (New York: Delacorte Press, 2001), 293.

Commissioning

[1]Henri Nouwen, *Here and Now: Living in the Spirit* (New York: The Crossroads Publishing Company, 1994), 65–67.

[2]Arundhati Roy, "Come September," in *The Impossible Will Take a Little While: A Citizen's Guide to Hope in a Time of Fear,* ed. Paul Rogat Loeb (Cambridge: Basic Books, 2004), 239–40.

[3]Tukio Mishima, quoted in Paula Carino, *Yoga to Go: A Take-It-With-You Guide for Travelers* (New York: Sterling Publishing, 2004), 11.

[4]Chinese Poem, quoted in *Restoring At-Risk Communities: Doing It Together and Doing It Right,* ed. John M. Perkins (Grand Rapids, Mich.: Baker Books, 1995), 18.

[5]Henri J.M. Nouwen, "Living the Moment to the Fullest," in *Bread for the Journey: A Daybook of Wisdom and Faith* (New York: Harper Collins, 1997), January 5 entry.

[6]Winston Churchill, *A Roving Commission: My Early Life* (New York: C. Scribner's Sons, 1930), 60.

Vulnerability

[1]Arthur Waskow, "The Sukkah of Shalom," in *The Impossible Will Take a Little While: A Citizen's Guide to Hope in a Time of Fear,* ed. Paul Rogat Loeb (Cambridge: Basic Books, 2004), 106–7.

[2]Henry David Thoreau, *The Writings of Henry David Thoreau* (New York: Houghton Mifflin, 1906), 198.

[3]Archbishop Oscar Romero, *Voice of the Voiceless: The Four Pastoral Letters and Other Statements,* tr. Michael J. Walsh (Maryknoll, N.Y.: Orbis Books, 1985), 133.

[4]Ranier Maria Rilke, *Letters to a Young Poet,* tr. Stephen Mitchell (New York: Random House, 1984), 34.

[5]Henri J.M. Nouwen, *The Inner Voice of Love: A Journey Through Anguish to Freedom* (New York: Image Books, 1996), 16–18.

[6]Eduardo Galeano, interviewed by David Barsamian, in *The Progressive* (March 2002).

[7]Martin Luther King, Jr., "Letter from Birmingham City Jail," in *A Testament of Hope: The Essential Writings and Speeches of Martin Luther King, Jr.,* ed. James Melvin Washington (San Francisco: HarperSanFrancisco, 1986), 290.

[8]Henri J.M. Nouwen, *¡Gracias! A Latin American Journal* (San Francisco: Harper & Row, 1983), 17.

[9]Thomas Merton, "Letter to a Young Activist," in *Prophet in the Belly of a Paradox,* ed. Gerald Twomey (New York: Paulist Press, 1978).

[10]Nouwen, *¡Gracias!* (San Francisco: Harper & Row, 1983), 173.

Accompaniment

[1]Daphne Rose Kingma, *True Love: How to Make Your Relationship Sweeter, Deeper and More Passionate* (York Beach, Maine: Conari Press, 2003), 3.

[2]Norman Maclean, *A River Runs Through It* (Chicago: University of Chicago Press, 1989), 2–3.

[3]Mother Teresa, *A Simple Path,* comp. Lucinda Varney (New York: Ballantine Books, 1995), 101.

[4]Douglas Wood, *Paddle Whispers* (Minneapolis: University of Minnesota Press, 1993), 49.

[5]Nicholas Wolterstorff, *Lament for a Son* (Grand Rapids, Mich.: William B. Eerdmans, 1987), 96–97.

[6]Saint Augustine of Hippo, quoted by Desmond Tutu in "The Prodigal God," in *God at 2000,* ed. Marcus Borg and Ross Mackenzie (Harrisburg, Pa.: Morehouse Publishing, 2000), 131.

[7]Thich Nhat Hanh, quoted by Pam Houston in *Sight Hound: A Novel* (New York: W.W. Norton & Company, 2005), 108.

[8]Heidi Neumark, *Breathing Space: A Spiritual Journey in the South Bronx* (Boston: Beacon Press, 2003), 98.

[9]Ibid., 223.

[10]Dinah Maria Mulock Craik, *A Life for a Life* (New York: Harpers, n.d.).

[11]Elie Wiesel, "Nobel Peace Prize Acceptance Speech," December 10, 1986, found at http://www.eliewieselfoundation.org/nobelprizespeech.aspx.

[12]Mary-Wynne Ashford, "Staying the Course," in *The Impossible Will Take a Little While: A Citizen's Guide to Hope in a Time of Fear,* ed. Paul Rogat Loeb (New York: Basic Books, 2004), 329.

[13]Tony Kushner, "Despair Is a Lie We Tell Ourselves," in *The Impossible Will Take a Little While: A Citizen's Guide to Hope in a Time of Fear,* ed. Paul Rogat Loeb (Cambridge: Basic Books, 2004), 170.

[14]Barbara Kingsolver, *Small Wonder* (New York: Harper Collins, 2002), 250–51.

Hospitality

[1]Alla Renee Bozarth, "Belonging," in *This Mortal Marriage: Poems of Love, Lament and Praise* (Lincoln, Nebr.: iUniverse, 2003), 172.

[2]Mother Teresa, *A Simple Path,* comp. Lucinda Vardey (New York: Ballantine Books, 1995), xxxiv.

[3]Wade Davis, *The Ethnosphere and the Academy,* keynote speech given at Penn State's Interinstitutional Consortium for Indigenous Knowledge Conference 2004. Manuscript retrieved online at http://www.ed.psu.edu/icik/2004ConferenceProceedings.html on January 3, 2008, pages 1, 13.

[4]Dorothy Day, *Loaves and Fishes* (Maryknoll, N.Y.: Orbis Books, 1963), 176.

[5]Starhawk, *Dreaming the Dark: Magic, Sex & Politics* (Boston: Beacon Press, 1982), 92.

Brokenness

[1]Thomas Merton, *Thoughts in Solitude* (New York: Farrar, Straus & Cudahy, 1956), 83.

[2]Eduardo Galeano, "Celebration of the Human Voice," in *The Impossible Will Take a Little While: A Citizen's Guide to Hope in a Time of Fear,* ed. Paul Rogat Loeb (Cambridge: Basic Books, 2004), 126.

[3]Yann Martel, *Life of Pi* (Orlando: Harcourt, 2001), 161.

[4]Bob Moorehead, "The Paradox of Our Age," in *Words Aptly Spoken* (Overlake Press, 1995).

[5]Martel, *Life of Pi,* 222–23.

[6]Desmond Tutu, "No Future Without Forgiveness," in *The Impossible Will Take a Little While: A Citizen's Guide to Hope in a Time of Fear,* ed. Paul Rogat Loeb (New York: Basic Books, 2004), 395.

[7]Heather Scheiwe, "Embracing Your Beauty, Moving in Strength," in *My Red Couch: And Other Stories on Seeking a Feminist Faith,* ed. Claire Bischoff and Rachel Gaffron (Cleveland: The Pilgrim Press, 2005), 36.

[8]Anne Lamott, *Plan B: Further Thoughts on Faith* (New York: Riverhead Books, 2005), 37.

[9]Henri J.M. Nouwen, *¡Gracias! A Latin American Journal* (San Francisco: Harper & Row, 1983), 130–31.

Grace

[1]Henri Nouwen, "The Path of Peace," in *Finding My Way Home: Pathways to Life and the Spirit* (New York: Crossroad, 2001).

[2]Jane Kenyon, as quoted in John H. Timmerman, *Jane Kenyon: A Literary Life* (Wm. B. Eerdmans, 2002), epigraph.

[3]Terry Anderson, *Den of Lions: Memoirs of Seven Years* (New York: Crown Publishers, 1993), 99.

[4]Howard Zinn, "The Optimism of Uncertainty," in *The Impossible Will Take a Little While: A Citizen's Guide to Hope in a Time of Fear,* ed. Paul Rogat Loeb (Cambridge: Basic Books, 2004), 64.

[5]Anne Brashares, *The Second Summer of the Sisterhood* (New York: Delacorte Press, 2003), 13–15.

[6]Jack Nichols, *Men's Liberation: A New Definition of Masculinity* (New York: Penguin, 1975), 85, quoted in James B. Nelson, *Embodiment: An Approach to Sexuality and Christian Theology* (Minneapolis: Augsburg Press, 1978), 90.

[7]Jhumpa Lahiri, *Interpreter of Maladies: Stories* (New York: Houghton Mifflin, 1999), 198.

[8]Peter Gabriel, "In Your Eyes," from the album *So* (Geffen Records, 1986), track 9.

[9]Peter Kreeft, *Heaven: The Heart's Deepest Longing* (San Francisco: Ignatius Press, 1989), 172.

[10]Sara Groves, "The One Thing I Know," from the album *The Other Side of Something* (Integrity Media, 2004), track 1.

[11]Douglas Wood, *Paddle Whispers* (Minneapolis: University of Minnesota Press, 1993), 115.

[12]Thomas Merton, quoted in Marcus Borg, *The Heart of Christianity: Rediscovering a Life of Faith* (San Francisco: HarperSanFrancisco, 2003), 155.

Epilogue

[1]Nelson Mandela, *Long Walk to Freedom: The Autobiography of Nelson Mandela* (Boston: Back Bay Books, 1995).

[2]Archbishop Oscar Romero, "The Prayer of Oscar Romero," in Christoph Blumhardt, *Action in Waiting* (Farmington, Pa.: Plough Publishing, 1998), xxx–xxxi.

[3]Martin Luther King Jr., "Letter from Birmingham City Jail," in *A Testament of Hope: The Essential Writings and Speeches of Martin Luther King, Jr.,* ed. James Melvin Washington (San Francisco: HarperSanFrancisco, 1986), 296, 300.